• • • •

REGISTERED PLACES
OF NEW MEXICO

El Santuario de Nuestro Esquipulas
at Chimayo. New Mexico is a
sanctuary of special places.
Photograph by Cotton Mather.

◆ ◆ ◆ ◆

REGISTERED PLACES OF NEW MEXICO
The Land of Enchantment

◆ ◆ ◆ ◆

Cotton Mather

and George F. Thompson

NEW MEXICO GEOGRAPHICAL SOCIETY ◆ MESILLA

This book is the first volume in the *Registered Places of America* series, published by the New Mexico Geographical Society in cooperation with the Center for American Places of Mesilla, New Mexico, and Harrisonburg, Virginia.

Distributed by the University of New Mexico Press, 1720 Lomas Boulevard, N.E., Albuquerque, New Mexico 87131-1591 U.S.A.
(505) 277-2346; FAX: (503) 277-9270

Requests for permission to reproduce material from this book should be sent to the New Mexico Geographical Society, P.O. Box 1201, Mesilla, New Mexico 88046-1201, U.S.A.

The acid-free paper used in this book meets the minimum requirements of American National Standard for Information Sciences-Permanence of Paper for Printed Library Materials, ANSI Z39.48-1984.

Library of Congress Cataloging-in-Publication Data will be found at the end of this book.

ISBN 0-9643841-0-8

Our New Mexico history is more complicated
than most, and far more visible. . . .
It is to see our past that thousands
of tourists come to New Mexico.

John Brinckerhoff Jackson,
A Sense of PLACE, a Sense of TIME (1994)

CONTENTS

A MESSAGE TO THE READER

A FEW YEARS AGO, while conducting an educational field trip in New Mexico, we strolled through Taos on a quiet autumn morning before people were stirring. In passing by the Taos Inn near the plaza, or town square, we paused to observe two bronze plaques on the Inn's adobe wall signifying that this building is officially listed on the national and state registers in Washington, D.C., and Santa Fe.

Traditionally, in reviewing our past, the tendency of Americans and officials is to consider as important only those points known as "historic landmarks." But in pondering these plaques we reminded ourselves that it is not enough to consider only historic landmarks such as the Taos Inn as indicators of *place*. After all, the significance of *place* is in comprehending the interconnectedness of elements in our natural and humanly constructed worlds. And since *place* represents a composite of points (historic and otherwise) as they occur at any one site or in any one area, we believe it is essential that citizens and officials begin to appreciate, understand, and recognize the interrelationships of points as they are revealed on the landscape.

Let us consider, for example, a well-preserved windmill on the Great Plains near Roswell. To recognize only the windmill—historic though it may be—without making the necessary connections to the ranch that belongs to a family that is part of a community in a particular region with a particular climate, culture, and geography is to miss the significance of the meaning of *place*. So why is it that we seem bent on recognizing only points and on treating them like isolated museum pieces rather than as part of a living landscape?

Our attention is thus directed toward identifying the *official places* of New Mexico—urban, rural, and wild—for this book and for posterity. These places are meant to offer a broader perspective than do individual landmarks, so that you, the reader, can discover the diversity of places that make New Mexico's geography, history, and culture so unique. These official places, which are registered with the New Mexico Geographical Society, complement the historic landmarks already listed with the state and federal agencies.

In designating the official places of New Mexico—and in writing the stories about them—we took great care to consider aspects of geography, history, geomorphology, anthropology, architecture, and art. We drove thousands of miles to re-explore places known to us through decades of research and fieldwork in the region; we shared and tested observations and insights about New Mexico's special places with leading scholars, writers, artists, curators, archivists, and officials as well as with scores of residents from all walks of life; and we consulted a multitude of articles, books, and reports. We were able to resolve discordances of records, accounts, and interpretations as a result of this thorough examination of the literature and extensive work in the field.

In using this book, readers will notice that the sequence of registered places is neither alphabetical nor temporal. Rather, we introduce you to the state via the Santa Fe Trail at Raton Pass in the north and we say farewell in the old Hispanic town of La Mesilla in the south. There is a logic in the presentation of the material, however, and the reader may consult the index at the end of the book for cross-references.

Because many readers will select certain registered places to read as they design and follow their own travel through the state, we have deemed it important to repeat some information occasionally, such as the dates of the Pueblo Revolt. This allows you to consider relevant historical and geographical information as it occurs; readers who start at page one and proceed to the end of the book will note these repetitions. We have not felt obliged to present a complete overview of the state's history or geography, since many guidebooks on New Mexico are already available, including the invaluable WPA guide first published in 1940. Occasional references to other works of history, geography, art, and literature are provided, however, as guideposts to further reading.

It is our hope that by reading and learning about the registered places of New Mexico—and by exploring them firsthand—you will gain new insights into New Mexico's past and discover why New Mexico *is* the Land of Enchantment. As the renowned geographer Yi-Fu Tuan recently shared with us: "We humans are very much a mixture of realism and fantasy. And my special fondness for New Mexico is that there the mixture becomes very real for me." Indeed.

The message of New Mexico and its registered places is ahead of you in this book.

Cotton Mather and George F. Thompson
La Mesilla, Nuevo Mexico
315 years after the Pueblo Revolt

ACKNOWLEDGMENTS

The authors extend heartfelt thanks to LTC James R. "Jimmy" Britton, director of the New Mexico Military Institute's Alumni Association, for his valued assistance and courtesies; to Peter Goin of Reno, Augustus W. Janeway of Colorado Springs, Stuart Klipper of Minneapolis, and Joseph Courtney White of Santa Fe for use of their photographs; to Dr. Gyula Pauer, director of the University of Kentucky Cartographic Laboratory, for his artistic rendering of the map of New Mexico's registered places; to Carol P. Mishler of the Center for American Places for her assistance in preparing the manuscript; to Dr. Sarah K. Myers of Croton-on-Hudson for her sensitive copyediting; to Anders Richter of Santa Fe for advice and counsel; and to Glen Burris of Johns Hopkins University Press for his splendid design. The authors, also, gratefully acknowledge the North Star Foundation of Aspen and the Patrons and Friends of the New Mexico Geographical Society and Center for American Places, whose generous contributions helped to make possible this publication.

····

REGISTERED PLACES
OF NEW MEXICO

MAP OF NEW MEXICO

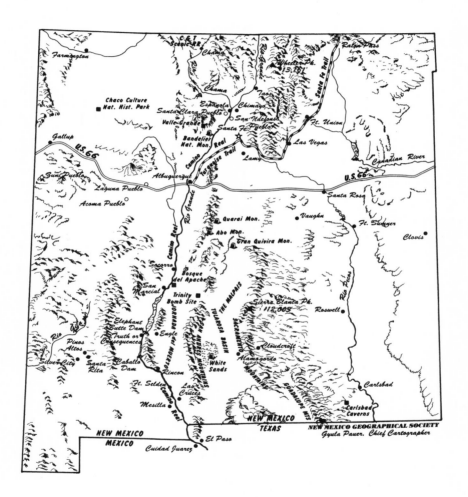

Farmington

C & T
Scenic RR
Chama

Chama

Wheeler Pk.
13,151

Raton Pass

Santa Fe Trail

Chaco Culture
Nat. Hist. Park

Española
Santa Clara Pueblo
Valle Grande

Chimayo
Taos

San Ildefonso
Santa Fe Pueblo

Ft. Union

Gallup

U.S. 66

Bandelier
Nat. Mon.

Camino Real

Turquoise Trail

Lamy

Las Vegas

Canadian River

Zuñi Pueblo

Albuquerque

U.S. 66

Laguna Pueblo

Santa Rosa

Acoma Pueblo

Quarai Mon.

Vaughn

Ft. Sumner

Clovis

Abo Mon.
Gran Quivira Mon.

Rio Grande

Camino Real

Socorro

Rio Pecos

Bosque
del Apache

San
Marcial

Trinity
Bomb Site

THE MALPAIS

Sierra Blanca Pk.
112,003

Roswell

TULAROSA BASIN

Elephant
Butte Dam
Truth or
Consequences

Engle

SACRAMENTO MOUNTAINS

Cloudcroft

Rio

Pinos
Altos

SAN ANDRES MOUNTAINS

White
Sands

Alamogordo

Silver City

Caballo
Dam

Santa
Rita

Rincon

BIG SNOWIE MTS.

Carlsbad

Ft. Selden

Las
Cruces

Carlsbad
Caverns

Mesilla

Camino Real

NEW MEXICO
TEXAS

NEW MEXICO GEOGRAPHICAL SOCIETY
Gyula Pauer. Chief Cartographer

NEW MEXICO
MEXICO

Cuidad Juarez

El Paso

The Santa Fe Trail • • • •

Today most visitors enter New Mexico from the northeast via Raton Pass over the old route of the Santa Fe Trail. The major natural impediment of the entire Santa Fe Trail — from Missouri to New Mexico — was surmounted at Raton Pass (elevation 7,834 feet) between Trinidad, Colorado, and Raton, New Mexico. It was the most critical and vivid part of the entire route, and it remains so today.

In 1821, the year in which Spain acknowledged the independence of Mexico, Captain William Becknell and four companions freighted goods on packhorses from Missouri to Santa Fe. The next year Becknell, who became known as the "Father of the Santa Fe Trail," with twenty-one men and three wagons, rolled west over the grama and buffalo grass of the Great Plains, through Raton Pass and on to Santa Fe.

Becknell's journey was the initiation of the Santa Fe Trail, one of the greatest continental lifelines to the West, and to a Spanish provincial capital whose Palace of the Governors was completed a decade before the Pilgrims landed on Plymouth Rock in Massachusetts (see page 43). Prior to 1822, however, New Mexico, then under Spanish rule, faced south, and traffic plied over the Camino Real de Tierra Adentro (Royal Road of the Interior Country) to Chihuahua and onward to Mexico City; Santa Fe trade to the east was forbidden. Therefore, the Santa Fe Trail provided a major directional change for New Mexico: away from Mexico to the south, toward Missouri and the east and a new orientation to American commerce and culture.

The Santa Fe Trail began on the west bank of the Missouri River at Franklin, Missouri; later, Independence be-

Raton Pass, historic pass and high point of the Santa Fe Trail at the Colorado-New Mexico border, has been used successively by covered wagons, a railroad, and federal highways. Photograph by Cotton Mather.

OF RELATED INTEREST: *Commerce of the Prairies*, by Josiah Gregg (1844).

came the starting point. The trail was the route of rapidly expanding trade until the Civil War. The estimated commodity value of $450,000 in 1843 ballooned to $5,000,000 in 1855. In 1860 more than 3,000 wagons, 9,000 men and women, 6,000 mules, and 27,000 oxen trundled over this route. Most of the movement was during the warm season, and the trip took about forty to sixty days. A monthly stage line, which operated from Independence to Santa Fe, was established in 1850. When the stagecoach and freight wagons arrived at the La Fonda Inn in Santa Fe, liquor flowed and certain women were joyous. The covered wagons were replaced with improved Conestogas and Murphys, and these vehicles were the major carriers until the railroad arrived. The first locomotive went over Raton Pass on 7 December 1878 (only sixty-three years before Pearl Harbor); in the fall of 1879 the 2,000-

foot-long Raton Tunnel (*raton* in Spanish means mouse) was opened, and Santa Fe was reached by rail on 9 February 1880. So the Santa Fe Trail was used by wagon trains and stagecoaches, later by the railroad, and today by cars and trucks on Interstate 25.

Congress recognized the route's significance in 1987 by establishing the Santa Fe National Historic Trail, which is administered by the National Park Service. Some tourists are beguiled into visiting Fort Union in order to see the trail. The trail is barely visible at Fort Union, even though the Civil War fort was a major supply depot and a military garrison for defense against a Confederate attack.

Route 66 ◆ ◆ ◆ ◆

In 1946 musician Bobby Troup wrote a song that etched U.S. Highway 66 indelibly on the map and in the minds of Americans: "If you ever plan to motor west; travel my way, take the highway that's the best. Get your kicks on Route Sixty-Six."

Route 66 has become such an icon of American culture and of motoring west that even today, despite its disappearance on much of the landscape, well-meaning senators and congressional representatives discuss seriously how to make the road a national historic landmark and once again a viable highway. Boosterism, which helped to create the road, is alive and well.

Route 66 came late as a trans-western roadway; in fact, it was officially approved as part of the National Highway Act only in 1926. In the roaring twenties, most major highways in the United States were aligned in a general east-to-west direction, reflecting the propensity of Americans to migrate coast-to-coast in similar latitudinal strategies. But U.S. 66 is different: its route is from Chicago to Albuquerque to Los Angeles in a more diagonal direction. Why is this so?

Three general opinions offer insight. First, Cyrus Stevens Avery, a prominent citizen and businessman from Tulsa, Oklahoma, was a booster of not only a much-

Scenes such as this one – with the baking ovens, scooter, basketball court, and vernacular buildings – are available to visitors who stroll through pueblos such as Isleta. Isleta Pueblo is on the original section of Route 66 about thirteen miles south of Albuquerque. Photograph by George F. Thompson.

needed national system of improved roads, but also a major national highway to Tulsa and through his native state, where road travel was miserable and a disincentive to growth and progress. Avery was a key player in the National Highway Act and, importantly, in designating the route for u.s. 66, seeing that the road was paved, and organizing the associations that publicized and developed the road and the tourist industry. Second, Route 66 conveniently paralleled existing rail lines for all but 160 miles, following the Chicago, Rock Island, & Pacific Railroad tracks southwest from Chicago to Santa Rosa, New Mexico, and then the Atcheson, Topeka & Santa Fe tracks west of Laguna Pueblo to Los Angeles; u.s. 60, known as the Ocean-to-Ocean Highway, from Norfolk, Virginia, to Los Angeles, had also followed a generally similar route

At Gallup, New Mexico (elevation 6,515 feet), one sees historic downtown U.S. 66 as it really was like in yesteryear. The prototype of railroad towns along U.S. 66 included, on one side of the highway, the railroad tracks and depot and, on the other side of the highway, the old hotels, a bank or two, and shops oriented to the tourist trade. A dynamic new mayor renamed Gallup "the Indian jewelry capital of America"; formerly it was known as "the Indian capital of America." Downtown one still finds Indian trading shops galore: retail, wholesale, jobber, and pawn. Photograph by Cotton Mather.

west of Springfield, Missouri, a generation earlier. Third, the need for a national highway between the national rail center in Chicago and the emerging metropolis of Los Angeles only confirmed the writing on the wall – that Los Angeles would become, within another generation, to the American West and Pacific Rim what New York City had always been to the East Coast and trans-Atlantic market.

And what of Route 66 in New Mexico, as it extends from the Great Plains in the east to the Colorado Plateau in the west? Much of the original highway is abandoned, having been replaced by Interstate 40. But there remain vestiges of the past that visitors can follow, remnants for slower travel. One of the more impressive segments is the original (1926) turn of Route 66 at Albuquerque, which parallels the Rio Grande south to Isleta Pueblo and to Los Lunas, and then heads northwest on N.M. 6 to where old 66 unites with Interstate 40 just east of Laguna Pueblo.

But perhaps the most appropriate section remains the stretch of interstate highway west of Laguna, where the road's path parallels the Santa Fe tracks all the way to Gallup and beyond. Here we can imagine the days of the Depression, when people desperately out-of-work headed west to the promise of California; here we can appreciate the better days after World War II and the Korean War when people back at work had more leisure time to get in their cars and travel west, to the Pacific through a Land of Enchantment.

SUGGESTED READING:
The Grapes of Wrath, by John Steinbeck (1939).

Fort Sumner and Billy the Kid ◆ ◆ ◆

Colonel Kit (Christopher) Carson, in the winter of 1863-1864, rounded up 8,000 Navajo and herded them 400 miles eastward from their home on the Colorado Plateau, past the Southern Rockies, and over Great Plains terrain to Fort Sumner at Bosque Redondo (The Round Grove of Trees), on the banks of the Pecos River. This was the infamous Long Walk, a government scheme to mold the Na-

The Kid's grave. The historical marker states that Billy the Kid's tombstone was repeatedly stolen and recovered. How fitting! Photograph by Cotton Mather.

vajo into the American way of life and make them self-sustaining. Their crops failed for numerous reasons, including hail storms, drought, cutworms, soil salinization, and Comanche raids. One third of the Navajo perished and led to the conclusion in 1868 of a new treaty in which they were permitted to return to their homeland.

Fort Sumner's walls crumbled over time, and little of it remains. The Long Walk is a tragically significant part of American history, and the site of Fort Sumner is tragically barren. So one strolls just to the east, to Billy the Kid's grave. Heroic figures may loom large, but here is a deification of a desperado, who at age twenty-one had killed twenty-one men. William Bonney, alias Billy the Kid, was killed near here by Sheriff Pat Garrett on 14 July 1881. Billy the Kid now rests behind bars.

The campus of the University of New Mexico, in Albuquerque, is of particular interest for its beauty and significant architecture. This campus has a concordant architecture based upon its regional setting, a type now referred to
as Santa Fe Style. This style is an outgrowth of Pueblo architecture, modified by Spanish colonial influence. Santa
Fe Style got an early thrust and initial recognition not in
the state capital but on this campus. Although Dr. William
Tight, the university's first president (1901) and an admirer
of Pueblo architecture, first decreed that all new buildings
on the campus were to be of Pueblo style, Isaac Hamilton
Rapp and his major successor, John Gaw Meem, are the
people who are often credited with having established the
Santa Fe Style. Meem was the chief consulting architect of
the university from 1933 to 1959, and he designed several
of the institution's most impressive edifices. Thus, he is the
person frequently associated with making a style really
look like New Mexico.

This campus has artfully designed berms, aesthetic
landscaping, a large and attractive grass-bordered pond,
and exterior social spaces remarkably placed and inte-
grated amidst a most impressive array of regionally styled
buildings. The Maxwell Museum is on this campus and
will guide you into the past, which is so vital in comprehending the character of this state.

The Maxwell Museum contains one of the nation's
finest archaeological collections. The collection comprises
more than 2,000,000 artifacts and specializes in cultures
of the Southwest, from Anasazi times to the present. Particularly noteworthy are the collections of Indian Pueblo
ceramics and Navajo rugs and the photographic archive of
more than 250,000 images. The exhibits are mainly the-
matic and rotate from time to time.

The anthropology department of the University of New
Mexico is one of America's leading centers for anthropo-

ONE AUTHORITATIVE
VIEWPOINT: *Creator of the
Santa Fe Style,* by Carl D.
Sheppard (1988)

The renowned Maxwell Museum of Anthropology on the University of New Mexico campus, in Albuquerque, with its "Santa Fe Style" architecture. Photograph by Cotton Mather.

logical and archaeological research. The department was directed in the 1930s by famed Edgar Lee Hewitt, who obtained the services of Frank Hibben to establish a museum. Gilbert Maxwell, a Farmington, New Mexico, oil man, loaned the museum an 800-piece Navajo rug collection. Later he gave the museum 50,000 shares of Occidental Petroleum stock — worth millions of dollars. Hibben, also, endowed the museum with his personal collections and with other assets valued at an estimated $6,500,000. Now the museum is steadily expanding from additional bequests.

The museum sponsors lectures, field trips, and ethnic music and dance performances. This place will surely register your interest!

Chaco Canyon • • • •

The largest, most significant, and most complex archaeological ruins in our nation are in Chaco Culture National Historical Park. These ruins are in a remote canyon – the nearest town is sixty miles away – and the park which embraces the ruins is the only registered place of New Mexico that is inaccessible by modern highway. Chaco Culture National Historical Park is in the back country, and it thrusts you into a thousand years of our ancestral heritage.

The park, in the rincon of northwestern New Mexico, is a shallow canyon about ten miles long that has been eroded through a sandstone cap. The canyon floor, at 6,200 feet elevation, is in a desert area with an erratic annual precipitation that averages eight inches and a short frost-free period that extends from about May 8 to October 6. *Chaco* is a regional Spanish term meaning desert.

Despite the region's xeric environment, the ancient Anasazi culture began to flower here in the early A.D. 900s. The Anasazis tilled the lowlands, built great urban centers, and developed an impressive road network. They constructed multi-storey stone buildings and developed an urban complex of at least 400 centers by A.D. 1000.

A BEAUTIFUL BOOK:
*The Four-Cornered Falcon:
Essays on the Interior West and
the Natural Scene,* by Reg
Saner (1993).

Why was this great complex abandoned? Between 1130 and 1180 a severe drought occurred. Also, the region's resources had become overtaxed. The result was a gradual emigration to better-watered lands, such as those to the east at Bandelier in the Frijoles Canyon of the Pajarito Plateau (see page 53).

The Anasazis were skilled stone artisans. Pueblo Bonito is the best known of the various ruins. It was four storeys high and had more than 600 rooms and forty kivas. These and other great ruins in Chaco Canyon amplify our knowledge of the extent and nature of this remarkable cultural complex. Artifacts abound which indicate that the Anasazis here had a broad range of trade, perhaps including contacts with Mexico and the ancient Toltecs. Their road system was a sophisticated one, more than 400 miles long, which connected about seventy-five communities.

The amazing Pueblo Bonito in Chaco Canyon. Photograph by Cotton Mather.

Visitors who travel now over the rough and rocky roads leading to Chaco Canyon may yearn for a resumption of travel over those of the Anasazi. Be that as it may, you should include your own provisions of food and beverage as you trek into this fabulous cultural complex of yore.

Salinas Monuments

✦ ✦ ✦ ✦

Great urban centers – in the United States and around the world – typically develop along regional boundaries and represent interregional trading and commerce. This was true of the ancient metropolitan complex, with its thriving Indian settlements, in the Salinas Basin near present-day Mountainair (elevation 6,492; population 926). Here was a rich assembly of Indian pueblos, with more than 10,000

Four views of Quarai, a Salinas National Monument. Photographs by George F. Thompson (top left) and by Cotton Mather.

residents, at the time the first Spanish explorers and missionaries arrived on the scene in 1598.

These "Native Americans" had long developed this area into a major trading center between the nomadic tribes of the Plains to the east and the sedentary villages along the Rio Grande to the west. They mined salt (*salina* means sa-

line) from nearby lake deposits and used it – in addition to farm products, cotton goods, and piñon nuts – as a commodity in trade for bison meat, hides, shells, and other goods between the two regions.

The Spanish missionaries failed to recognize the sophisticated nature of local culture, commerce, religion, and art. Instead, they wasted no time trying to control and convert the Indians to Christianity and to exploit the converts' labor into building missions and churches. Such exploitation created a wee bit of strife; that, combined with disease and drought, and with more frequent attacks by the Apache and Comanche, caused the Indians to leave their ancient Salinas villages by the 1670s. In 1680 the Spanish were driven from all of New Mexico by the Pueblo Revolt, only to return permanently twelve years later.

SUGGESTED READING:
Death Comes for the Archbishop, by Willa Cather (1927).

Three of the largest Salinas pueblos, with their accompanying seventeenth-century Spanish missions, have been preserved as the Salinas National Monuments: Abo, Quarai, and Gran Quivira. Ruins of these three urban nodes are relatively unknown to the American public, yet they are among the most impressive and significant archaeological sites in the Southwest.

New Mexico Military Institute ◆ ◆ ◆ ◆

The American South has long had a rich tradition of military service that is, in part, reflected in its military schools – from private military academies, to thriving ROTC programs at public high schools and state universities, to renowned military colleges such as The Citadel in South Carolina and Virginia Military Institute in Lexington. It is not surprising, then, to learn that one of the South's most distinguished military institutions is in New Mexico, on the Great Plains, in Roswell.

New Mexico Military Institute, a state-supported institution founded in 1891, has, since 1909, received the distinction of being one of the ten most distinguished mili-

The Rock Garden and statue of "The Bronco" at New Mexico Military Institute in Roswell before the Headquarters Building was erected in 1940. Alligators then lived in the pond. Photograph courtesy of the Alumni Association of NMMI.

The new Bronco at NMMI. The barracks in the background are reminiscent of the military Gothic architecture at Virginia Military Institute in the Shenandoah Valley. Photograph by George F. Thompson.

tary schools in the nation, as accorded by the War Department of Defense. In 1956 the academic curriculum was changed and ever since has included a four-year college preparatory and two-year college education. NMMI became co-educational in 1977.

Among NMMI's distinguished alumni are journalist Sam Donaldson, artist Peter Hurd, whose museum is in San Patricio, fifty miles to the west of Roswell on U.S. 70, former quarterback of the Dallas Cowboys and business-man Roger Staubach, Lieutenant General Hobart R. Gay, who was General George Patton's Chief of Staff during World War II, and three Pulitzer Prize winners: Dr. Ira B. Harkey, Jr., Paul Horgan, a two-time winner, and Thomas H. Thompson.

In visiting NMMI you cannot help but be impressed by the campus architecture and grounds. In fact, you may notice a striking resemblance to the campus of Virginia Military Institute. This is no accident. Colonel James W. Willson, who served as superintendent of NMMI from 1901 to 1916, graduated from VMI in 1894, recruited VMI graduates to occupy important positions, and helped to inaugurate a building campaign that reflected VMI's architectural tradition of the military Gothic style.

In visiting Roswell (elevation 3,557 feet; population 47,397) you will be impressed by the town's appearance and citizenry. Even during the hard times of the 1930s it was observed, in the WPA guidebook, *New Mexico*, that Roswell is "one of the most modern and attractive cities in the State with miles of wide, paved streets shaded by fine old cottonwoods and willows, and attractive homes, gardens, and public buildings." This is equally true of Roswell today.

OF RELATED INTEREST:
The Days of the Cattleman,
by Earnest Staples Osgood
(1929).

It is also worth noting that the Pecos River valley was prized for its grama grass, which made for an excellent route for cattle drives from Texas to forts in New Mexico and Colorado and beyond during the mid-nineteenth century. Thus, Main Street in Roswell was built extra wide so the cattle herds could pass through with ease.

Bosque del Apache ◆ ◆ ◆ ◆

One of the greatest waterfowl and wildlife sanctuaries in the entire nation is eighteen miles south of Socorro: Bosque del Apache (elevation 4,500 feet). The Rio Grande courses through it.

Bosque del Apache is part of a national wildlife refuge program that began during the Theodore Roosevelt presidency when Pelican Island in Florida was established in 1903. These early refuges were set aside, at least initially, for the preservation of one or more endangered species, and they soon served as prime breeding areas and as great resting and feeding stops along major flyways. Portions of some refuges became designated as wilderness areas, too.

A prime reason Bosque del Apache National Wildlife Refuge was created was to help save the then imperiled

Tens of thousands of snow geese congregate and rest at Bosque del Apache before they head north to Canada for the summer. Photograph by Augustus W. Janeway.

sandhill crane (*Grus canadensis*), a stately bird once valued only for its plumage. The sandhill is no longer endangered, thanks to environmental law, research, and conservation efforts at Bosque and other wildlife reserves in the United States and Canada. Today visitors at Bosque can see, during the peak wintertime season, 10,000 sandhills, 39,000 snow geese, and 50,000 ducks, give or take a few, among other undocumented migrants. Herons, hawks, egrets, and eagles can be seen year-round. A few whooping cranes (*Grus americana*) now winter at Bosque as well. The whooper is one of the world's most endangered birds today. Of the 250 left, only 150 are wild.

The Civilian Conservation Corps began the work of creating the refuge after the U.S. government purchased the Bosque del Apache Land Grant in 1936. The CCC constructed water impoundments and diverted Rio Grande water into irrigation channels to supply the artificial ponds and marshes. The refuge currently comprises 57,191 acres, of which 30,287 are in wilderness areas. Plans are under way to expand the refuge. Approximately 320 bird species have been sighted since 1940 in addition to about 400 different mammals, reptiles, and amphibians, among them coyote, fox, badger, bobcat, porcupine, rattlesnake, mule deer, wild turkey, and the soft-shelled turtle. The park is open to visitors year-round. Wintertime is the best season for viewing the sandhills, snow geese, ducks, and other migratory fowl; the best viewing times are at dawn and dusk.

Bosque del Apache has an inspired cooperative farm program which allows local farmers to use more than 1,400 acres of refuge land on a crop-share basis: one-third of the corn grown on the refuge is left in fields for wildlife and two-thirds is harvested by the farmers for personal use. The irrigated farmlands are very productive. Alfalfa is, also, grown in this part of the Rio Grande valley, as silage for beef and dairy cattle. These fields of green are visible as one drives the nine miles south on N.M. 1 from San Antonio to the Bosque refuge.

OF RELATED INTEREST:
Great River: The Rio Grande in North American History, two volumes, by Paul Horgan (1954).

Bosque del Apache is part of the largest continuous cottonwood *(alamosa)* bosque in the United States, an area that extends from Elephant Butte Lake (see page 23), fifty miles to the south, to Cochiti Lake, 135 miles to the north. *Bosque* means a forest or woods; in New Mexico it refers specifically to riverine thickets of large trees. Today alamosa are not generating well in this Rio Grande bosque because of river channelization, which deprives the trees of a natural water flow. Compounding this problem are exotics such as salt cedar *(Tamarix)*, Siberian elm, and Russian olive trees, which are aggressive and excessively thirsty and overwhelm the native cottonwood groves.

The Fish and Wildlife Service, which administers Bosque del Apache, is trying to deal with these problems. But on the horizon is another matter: New Mexico is booming, and Rio Grande water is becoming more precious. It remains to be seen whether the national interests of preserving and expanding the bird sanctuary will complement or conflict with local and regional concerns for agricultural and urban use that will likely arise about the supply of Rio Grande water.

The Jornada del Muerto • • • •

The Jornada del Muerto, or Journey of Death, was a Spanish colonial road through one of the most awesome areas of the Southwest. It was the most challenging and death-defying segment of the Camino Real de Tierra Adentro, or the Royal Road of the Interior Country, which connected Mexico City and Santa Fe via Zacatecas, Chihuahua, Ciudad Juarez, La Mesilla, and Albuquerque. The route of this colonial road through Nuevo Mexico followed closely the Rio Grande with one major exception, that stretch from Rincon to San Marcial. The Spanish caravans gratefully utilized the green band of forage and Rio Grande water for their livestock and human components. Less appreciated were the Apache attacks and problems of periodic inundation along certain bands of riverine bottomlands. So the Camino Real departed from the Rio Grande valley at Rincon and rejoined it about ninety miles to the north at San Marcial.

The southern entrance of this ninety-mile-long trek away from the Rio Grande was through a broad gap between the Caballo Mountains (elevation to 6,091 feet) on the north and the Sierra de Las Uvas (elevation to 6,294 feet) on the south. The journey northward was through a broad arid basin bordered by the Caballo Mountains and the Fra Cristobal Range (elevation to 6,223 feet) on the west and the San Andres Mountains (elevation to 8,239 feet) and the Oscura Mountains (elevation to 8,640 feet) on the east. It was in this basin, at the Trinity Site, that the world's first atomic bomb was exploded on 16 July 1945.

The only water in or near this arid basin was in a steep canyon in the Fra Cristobal Range and sporadically in the Laguna del Muerto (Lake of Death), a playa with saline,

The Jornada del Muerto at Engle, with vineyards and the San Andres Mountains in the background. Photograph by Cotton Mather.

unpotable water present only after rain. The average annual precipitation in the basin is about eight inches; more than half of that occurs in the hot months of July, August, and September, when evaporation is excessive. The Spanish were unaware of the subsurface water resource. In 1871, however, a 160-foot-deep well penetrated to water seeping outward from the base of the mountains.

This arid depression is actually a series of subbasins separated by barely discernible divides of unconsolidated alluvium which in places is more than 300 feet deep. Bajadas (compound peidmont alluvial fans) dominate the eastern portion of the Jornada del Muerto basin area, while an extensive pediment is present on the west. The Rio Grande poured through this basin in late Tertiary time, but was shifted to its present course by structural displacement and igneous activity.

The basin of the Jornada del Muerto is a synclinal structure whose alluvial surface has a general southward slope of about forty-two inches per mile and a general floor elevation of about 4,600 feet. The basin has few physical features aside from some recent geologic flows, playas (intermittent saline ponds or lakes), alkali flats, and xerophytic plants. Although cacti, creosote bush, and mesquite are present now, grasses were more evident a century ago and supported some ranching. Livestock and human beings perished along this Spanish colonial trail – so many that, if the human graves were evenly spaced, it is claimed that one grave would mark the trail every 500 feet.

Today three points on the map highlight the route of the trail: Rincon at the south, Engle at a midpoint, and San Marcial at the north all are along the Santa Fe Railway, which follows the general path of the old caravan route of the Jornada del Muerto.

Rincon is a moribund village at the junction of the north-south line of the Santa Fe Railway with a branch line leading southwest to Deming. Once important as a railway center, its functions have largely atrophied.

Engle, eighteen miles east of Truth or Consequences (known as Hot Springs prior to 1950) and accessible by paved highway, began in 1880 as a shipping station and mining-supply base. It had two stage lines, two general stores, and an all-night restaurant. It continued until about 1900 as a cattle-shipping station. Now only a few buildings remain, but the view around Engle of the Jornada del Muerto is good and unobstructed. In the late 1980s economic aspirations were revived as European viticulturists had water piped in from Elephant Butte Lake and developed extensive vineyards and huge wineries near Engle. Visitors to Engle, with yearnings for civilization and cold cerveza, will return to Truth or Consequences or remain at a dead end road.

San Marcial was reached by the Santa Fe Railway in 1880. In the 1920s it had a population of several thousand. A Fred Harvey restaurant of the nationally famous chain was established there in 1883 and it closed in 1929. In the

1920s two floods by the Rio Grande wreaked havoc on
San Marcial. The one in September of 1929 completely de-
molished the city, adding a new twist to the meaning of
Jornada del Muerto.

Elephant Butte Dam and Lake

• • • •

Hydrohistorians view the Elephant Butte Dam as one of
the world's great engineering structures. It was completed
in 1916 as an impoundment of water of Rio Grande water,
and it cost only $5,000,000 to construct. It was then the
largest dam in the United States and held more water than
any other irrigation reservoir in the world. The dam is
306 feet high, 1,674 feet long, and has a spillway elevation
of 4,450 feet. It impounds 2,200,000 million acre-feet,
enough to cover Delaware, the "First State," to a depth of
two feet; it also covers the old U.S. Army post of Fort
McRae.

The lake behind the dam is thirty-six miles long, has a
maximum width of three miles and a 200-mile-long shore-
line, and inundates sixty square miles. This water body is
one of the best fishing lakes in America, and it is a favorite
mecca for sailboating and powerboating. The island of Elephant Butte is a volcanic neck near the dam and state
park.

Caballo Dam, eleven miles south of Elephant Butte
Dam, was completed in 1938. It impounds about 300,000
acre-feet and has a spillway elevation of 4,204 feet.

The Elephant Butte Dam was built under a treaty with
Mexico because the water also irrigates Mexican lands. On
the lower Rio Grande, near the Gulf of Mexico, most of
the irrigated land is on the American side, but much of the
water comes from Mexican tributaries of the Rio Grande.
The Rio Grande Compact among New Mexico, Texas, and
Colorado established that 790,000 acre-feet annually
would be released. But since 1952 the project has only received annually about 600,000 acre-feet!

The Elephant Butte Dam was
completed in 1916, the same year
the National Park Service was
established. The attractive dam,
with its elegant lampposts, is still
holding up under increased
pressures for more water. Back in
the teens, engineers pondered a
different aesthetic. Photograph by
Cotton Mather.

OF RELATED INTEREST:
*Report of the Lands of the Arid
Region of the United States,* by
John Wesley Powell (1879).

This romantic view of Elephant Butte Lake with its pleasure boats may remind some poets and water skiers of places more foreign than New Mexican. Photograph by Cotton Mather.

The Elephant Butte Dam and the irrigation project have essentially been paid for. Indeed, they have been a gratifyingly sound economic and social investment. The approximate $4,000,000 of annual expenses are mostly for administrative costs and for maintenance of the facilities, including those of the irrigation canal and ditch system.

Sierra Blanca ♦ ♦ ♦ ♦

The high point of the Sacramento Mountains and the Mescalero Apache region is Sierra Blanca, elevation 12,003 feet. From the ground and from the air, Sierra Blanca towers over the Mescalero Apache Reservation, over the White Mountain Wilderness Area of the Lincoln National Forest, and over White Sands and the Tularosa Basin. The greatest topographic relief in New Mexico is from the Tularosa Ba-

sin (elevation of about 4,000 feet) to the crest of Sierra
Blanca.

Sierra Blanca is, significantly, 161 miles south of Santa
Fe, which puts it 161 miles south of the Rocky Mountains.
It is, therefore, the southernmost point in the Interior West
with a major ski resort and the southernmost point in the
United States on which Arctic lifezone conditions exist.
With amenities for year-round recreation and proximity to
Albuquerque, Las Cruces, Roswell, and Santa Fe – in addi-
tion to Texas and northern Mexico – Sierra Blanca and the
Sacramento Mountains offer a natural refuge for outdoor
enthusiasts and visitors from all over the state and the re-
gion.

Historically, Sierra Blanca has had spiritual importance
for the Mescalero Apache, who have deemed the mountain
life-giving and sacred. In recent times, however, the Mescaleros also have looked to their lofty mountain as an op-
portunity to reduce chronic unemployment on their reservation and to provide a means for greater tribal self-
sufficiency.

In 1960 the u.s. Forest Service granted a thirty-year
lease to a non-Indian corporation to develop and operate a
ski area a few thousand feet below Sierra Blanca's summit.
In 1963, with the aid of $1,250,000 of federal money, the
Mescaleros purchased the Sierra Blanca Ski Resort and renamed it Ski Apache in the mid-1980s. Today hundreds of
thousands of skiers annually seek its fine powder to enjoy
runs on the forty-plus trails.

The Mescaleros, under the leadership of tribal chief
Wendell Chino and again with taxpayer money, have also
been able to create, own, and operate a first-class resort on
the reservation. Known as the Inn of the Mountain Gods
(elevation 7,200 feet), it opened in 1975. The impressive,
modern complex of buildings overlooks the attractive, 120-
acre artificial Lake Mescalero, and the Inn's tennis courts
and golf course are ranked among the twenty-five best for
resorts by leading golf and tennis magazines. Many of the
Inn's employees are Mescaleros.

The Inn of the Mountain Gods, a Mescalero Apache enterprise, with Sierra Blanca in the background. Photograph by George F. Thompson.

The Mescalero Apache Reservation was established in 1872, and the present boundaries for its 460,000 acres were determined by 1883. All lands in the reservation are owned in common by the nearly 3,000 tribal members; a tribal council administers these lands. The tribe pays no government taxes; neither do individuals, except for property taxes. There are six major Apache groups, the Mescalero Tribe included.

Ski Apache and the Inn of the Mountain Gods have been financial winners for the Mescaleros, especially after professional management was secured to assist in their operation. Timber cutting, cattle ranching, and a national fish hatchery contribute as well to the Mescalero economy.

The Cumbres & Toltec Scenic
Railroad at Chama. It is best
to call ahead for reservations,
especially in the fall. Photograph
by Cotton Mather.

The Cumbres & Toltec
Scenic Railroad   ◆ ◆ ◆ ◆

The Cumbres & Toltec Scenic Railroad is America's long-
est and highest narrow-gauge steam railroad. It was started
in 1880 as an extension of the Denver & Rio Grande Railroad, built to serve rich mining camps in the San Juan
Mountains of Colorado. The railroad track and equipment
were jointly purchased by the states of Colorado and
New Mexico in 1970 for $547,120. The sixty-four-mile-
long route extends from Chama, New Mexico, to Antonito,
Colorado. Trains depart daily, from depots at either end,
between mid-May and mid-October. Travel can be by
round-trip rail or one-way by rail and return by auto van.
Parallel to the rail route is New Mexico and Colorado
State Highway 17. Some travelers prefer to go by highway,
especially if they desire more flexibility for photography

Old 484, an original coal-fired locomotive of the Cumbres & Toltec Scenic Railroad, gets steamed near Cumbres Pass. Photograph by Cotton Mather.

stops; railway buffs, of course, choose the romance of travel by an old-time steam railroad.

The railroad and highway route is through some of America's wildest and most spectacular scenery. From Chama (elevation 7,850 feet), the train ascends four percent grades and goes through the gorgeous Toltec Gorge of the Los Pinos River, through numerous tunnels and over existing trestles, and across Cumbres Pass (elevation 10,022 feet), to Antonito (elevation 7,888 feet). The trains are unheated, but are equipped with restrooms and stop near midday at Osier for lunch. The finest time of year for scenic travel is in late September and early October, when the mountains are crested with snow and the golden-hued aspen contrast with the pine greenery.

Chama is an attractive old town that is popular with tourists, fishermen, and big-game hunters. It has modern

Cowboy Bill Baird, aged 45, on his horse Midnight, aged 8, at Cumbres Pass, northeast of Chama near the state border. Bill herds 2,600 head of cattle from May to the October roundup on government-permit land. During the winter he is a ski instructor at Red River, near Taos, at one of the premier ski resorts in the Rockies. Bill, originally from California, came *east* seeking a new way of life in the wide-open spaces of the Interior West. Photograph by Cotton Mather.

tourist facilities, an old railway depot, and the adjacent
Foster's Hotel and Restaurant, built in 1881. The post office, always a key element in determining a town's date of
official settlement, was established in 1880.

Las Vegas ••••

Las Vegas, originally named Nuestra Señora de los Dolores
de Las Vegas (Our Lady of Sorrows of the Meadows), has a
population of 15,068 and, despite plate tectonics, retains its
initial, official elevation of 6,391 feet. A settlement petition
was granted under the proviso that a plaza be included as a
market and meeting place and for protection against Indians who were hostile to such settlement. This became the
center of Old Town. After the railroad arrived, in the
1870s, New Town, now known as East Las Vegas, developed and became a nasty nest for rascal outlaws and cut-
throat gangs with such colorful characters as Web-
Fingered Smith, Hog Jones, Hatchet-Face Kit, Pawnee Bill,
and Tommy the Poet. The town's development included an
ample supply of saloons, dance halls, and bawdy houses.
Crime thrived, and hangings were popular social events.
By 1900 Las Vegas was the largest urban agglomeration in
New Mexico.

Tributary to Las Vegas, and five miles away, were the
hot springs bathhouse and Montezuma Hotel. The hotel
was constructed on the hot springs property that was purchased in 1879 by the Santa Fe Railway. After fires and
other difficulties, a 343-room edifice was built in 1888.
Here stayed – but fortunately not at the same time – such
guests as Teddy Roosevelt, Ulysses S. Grant, Kaiser
Wilhelm, and Emperor Hirohito. The Santa Fe Railway
closed the hotel in 1912 and donated the property to the
YMCA. Since then, in an ongoing educational experience,
the Baptists, the Archdiocese of Santa Fe, and the Armand
Hammer Foundation have squandered substantial funds in
this hot springs relic. Surprisingly, the federal government
has yet to take over the landmark.

Other kinds of distinctive architecture can be found in the railroad district of East Las Vegas,
including a Harvey House Hotel,
a 1920s gas station, and unique
building advertisements such as
the one pictured: "Calumet Says
Howdy: Where the Great Plains
Meet the Mighty Rockies." Photograph by George F. Thompson.

Handsome new buildings add to the attractive campus of New Mexico Highlands University in Las Vegas. Photograph by Cotton Mather.

Next, a note about higher education. Las Vegas takes justifiable pride in New Mexico Highlands University, which got its start with classes opening on 3 October 1898, fourteen years before statehood. Edgar Lee Hewitt – famed archaeologist, first director of the School of American Research, first director of the Museum of New Mexico, author of *Ancient Life in the American Southwest* (1930), and coauthor with Adolph Bandelier of *Indians of the Rio Grande Valley* (1937) – was the institution's first president. The student enrollment is about 2,800 on the seventy-five-acre campus near the city center. The architecture is predominantly stucco and tile roofed. The Ilfeld Auditorium, built in the early 1920s, is on the National Register of Historic Places. The curriculum is broadly based, but with notable attention paid to Spanish literature and Hispanic culture. Approximately forty percent of the faculty are

The Old Town plaza in Las Vegas still boasts a thriving hotel, a great bookstore, and other commercial enterprises housed in late-nineteenth-century historic splendor. Photograph by Cotton Mather.

Hispanic, and Gilbert Sanchez, the current president, is the third consecutive Hispanic leader of the institution.

Today Las Vegas has interstate highway access and Amtrak railroad service. It is one of the most remarkable repositories of architecture in the American West. Included are colonial compounds of adobe, buildings that sprouted with the arrival of the railroad, the structures that arose with the advent of Interstate 25, and the remarkably attractive campus of New Mexico Highlands University. The visitor will be delighted by the Old Town Plaza, with such notable structures around it as that which housed the First National Bank from 1888 to 1992 and the Plaza Hotel, built in 1881 and 1882 and recently renovated. A fine bookstore and old-fashioned pharmacy are also located there. Across the Galinas River, which flows through the center of Las Vegas, are such gems as the Carnegie Library,

The Carnegie Library in Las Vegas reminds scholars not only of Thomas Jefferson's magnificent home, Monticello, near Charlottesville, Virginia, but also of the power of architectural diffusion from the East into the Great West.

The library is located on one of Las Vegas's beautiful plazas. Handsome residential dwellings surround the square as if this were the Upper Middle West. Photograph by George F. Thompson.

built in 1903 and fashioned after Thomas Jefferson's Monticello in Virginia, and St. Paul's Episcopal Church. Main Street, near the old plaza, is showing signs of new growth, as businesses refurbish the old buildings and offer such fashionable items as antiques and exotic coffees. Santa Fe's presence some sixty miles to the west by interstate will no doubt continue to influence Las Vegas's future development and resident population.

The Turquoise Trail   • • • •

More than a recent promotional gimmick to connect dormant mining communities, the Turquoise Trail (old N.M. 10; now N.M. 14) is the modern name for the old road that connected Albuquerque and Santa Fe on the eastern side of the Sandia Mountains (elevation to 10,678 feet) before Interstate 25 was developed to the west. Although it is true that what one sees today is largely a museum tour of old mining and railroad towns – Golden, Madrid, and Los Cerrillos – the name is attributed to the high-quality turquoise that was mined in the Cerrillos Hills since prehistoric times. Coal, gold, lead, silver, and zinc were also hauled out of the mountains surrounding this scenic highway.

Golden, officially founded in 1879, was the site of the first gold rush west of the Mississippi after placer gold was discovered in 1825, and the attractive mission church, built in the late 1830s, still stands. Coal was discovered in Madrid (elevation 6,000 feet) in 1835, but it was 1869 before a company town was established. The Albuquerque and Cerrillos Coal Company had a record of comparatively steady production until operations shut down in 1959. The town even had tennis courts and a seven-hole golf course, but its mine tailings are a feature of the landscape today. Hippies and artisans were attracted to Madrid's cheap housing during the 1970s and 1980s and you can still see their ongoing restoration efforts. Los Cerrillos (Little Hills) is an ancient turquoise mining center and a former coal-

Los Cerrillos: Walt Disney could not have built a better Western set. Photograph by Cotton Mather.

mining community. Its railroad strip was built by the Atcheson, Topeka & Santa Fe Railway in 1879, and in its heyday in the 1880s civic pride included twenty-one saloons and four hotels. Today Cerrillos is best known as a site for movie making, rustic antique shops, authentic Western streets, and memorable church services on Sunday.

Santa Fe, to the north, and Albuquerque, to the south – the old terminus points for the road – are stretching their britches severely. One anticipates continued spillover growth and tourist traffic onto the Turquoise Trail. Occasionally there are rumors about future mining activity as well.

Albuquerque, founded in 1706 about a century after Santa
Fe, has, with its suburbs, more than a half million people.
The two largest New Mexican cities, Albuquerque and Las
Cruces, are the state's only cities that are individually accessible by two interstate highways, yet Las Cruces, with
its suburbs, has only 125,000 persons. This highlights the
dominance of Albuquerque in New Mexico's population
geography.

Tourism is New Mexico's second largest economic com-
ponent, and more than ninety percent of the tourists come
by automobile. When they arrive in Albuquerque, the
numero uno attraction is Old Town. So important is Old
Town that hotels and other tourist-oriented businesses ad-
vertise their location in terms of distance from it.

Old Albuquerque was on the significant trade route of
the Camino Real de Tierra Adentro, or the Royal Road of
the Interior Country, which connected Mexico City with
Santa Fe. Albuquerque was an important military post, and
people who settled there in the early 1700s sought protection from Indian attacks.

The center of old Albuquerque was the plaza around
which were commercial establishments and residences. Fac-
ing the plaza was the Church of San Felipe de Neri, under
construction in 1706. This has been replaced by the new
Church of San Felipe de Neri, begun in 1793, and the ad-
joining Sister Blandina Convent, constructed in 1881 for
nuns who taught in a nearby school.

Old Albuquerque, just east of the Rio Grande, was located on alluvial soils and with a major source of irrigation
water. Whereas the average annual precipitation is only 8.4
inches, the long annual frost-free season averages 198 days.
This compares with Jackson, Wyoming, and its annual
frost-free season of just forty-one days. Agriculture has
thrived in the Albuquerque area and, early on, greatly augmented growth.

New Albuquerque was platted in 1880, when the railroad was routed two miles to the east. This shifted

The new church with its formal, European-like garden faces the plaza in Albuquerque's Old Town. Construction of the church was undertaken in 1793, when George Washington was President of the United States. Photograph by Cotton Mather.

Albuquerque's main market functions to what is now "downtown"; Old Town remained as an ecclesiastical, social, and residential core for Spanish residents. New Albuquerque boomed and Old Town languished. When the Great Depression came, the county welfare office was located in Old Town – near the clientele.

Old Town, however, rejuvenated immediately after World War II. It became a major tourist attraction, for three basic reasons. First, Old Town retained many of its attractive, low, old Spanish structures built of adobe and with flat roofs. Second, Old Town became one of the Southwest's major artisan centers for jewelry, Navajo rugs, and handicrafts. Third, Old Town became noted for its festivals and its restaurants with Mexican culinary. The plaza, with its cottonwood trees, remains one of the Southwest's most attractive social settings; the central gazebo serves

This street scene near Old Town's plaza – with its galleries, shops, Territorial Style architecture, and second-storey *ristras* (strings of chiles) – is a favorite of post-card photographers and artists. Photograph by Cotton Mather.

as a stage for musicians and dancers, and the wrought-iron benches accommodate the informal audience.

Today Old Town has approximately 160 shops, galleries, and restaurants. The Covered Wagon, a long-established and widely known shop on the southwestern corner of the plaza, has some of the finest Indian-made silver ornaments and jewelry and one of the Southwest's best collections of fine pueblo pottery and Navajo rugs. Another special Old Town attraction, on the southeastern corner of the plaza, is La Placita Restaurant. This fifty-five-year-old restaurant is in the 290-year-old Armijo adobe residence and is famed for its New Mexican food. Under its long portal, which faces the plaza, Indians and local artisans display their wares. Most of the Indians are from Santo Domingo Pueblo. These Indians are superb silver and turquoise craftsmen, and they are the main traders of Pueblo jewelry and pottery.

Christmas Eve is the most memorable time to visit Old Town. Thousands of farolitas, known as luminarias in southern New Mexico, then line the sidewalks and adobe walls. You will long remember a visit to Old Town in this festive setting as the music of the season permeates to the very core of your being.

Canyon Road • • • •

Santa Fe is one of the major art centers in the United States, perhaps rivaled only by Los Angeles and New York City, and Canyon Road is the embodiment of the cultural *compage* that distinguishes this region. Within a few blocks on Canyon Road you can become immersed in the aesthetic and inspirational aspects of three great cultures – Indian, Hispanic, and Anglo. In all other regions of the United States, the Anglo culture overwhelmed what preceded it, at best leaving symbolic tokens of the past. Only in this region of America, centered on Santa Fe, has there not been an obliteration of past cultures by the Anglo advance.

Each of the three cultural groups here has been captivated by the physical and mystical charm of the region, and as time has passed each group has contributed to the evolving construct of the regional character. It is this unique aspect that is articulated particularly in the regional art. This art is expressed in the Santa Fe Style architecture (see page 8) as well as the jewelry, carved furniture, ceramics, sculpture, weavings, paintings, and even culinary tastes.

As you stroll along Canyon Road, bear in mind that it was once just a trail used by thirteenth-century Indians en route to the Pecos Pueblo to the east. But today, near the entrance of Canyon Road, you may visit the famed Fenn Gallery, with its serene garden and bronze sculptures, and then proceed eastward along Canyon Road past many

In the attractive garden of Fenn Gallery, near the entrance of Canyon Road in Santa Fe, you can experience the beauty of art and nature. Photograph by Cotton Mather.

other galleries, old adobe residences, small eateries, or into the Compound – Santa Fe's only four-star restaurant. The Cristo Rey Church, just east of Palace Avenue, is a must. The edifice was designed by the noted architect John Gaw Meem. Built with 180,000 adobe bricks by members of the congregation, it is one of the largest of all adobe buildings in the Southwest. Inside is an outstanding piece of ecclesiastical art, a thirty-two-foot-high, hand-carved altar screen that was made in 1760.

To keep Canyon Road in place, the city has officially designated it as "a residential arts and crafts zone." But you can take it with you as a lovely memory as you explore galleries with traditional and contemporary art.

The Palace of the Governors

・・・・

The Palace of the Governors, or Palacio Real, in Santa Fe, was completed in 1610. This is the oldest government building in the United States, and it is a monument to Spanish settlement in the American Southwest when our Eastern Seaboard was yet a frontier wilderness.

The Palace speaks volumes about Santa Fe as a place. For example, the WPA guidebook, *New Mexico*, aptly states that "this building is so old that some of its walls are constructed of puddled adobe, a technique typical of the pre-Columbian era. . . . Nowhere else in the United States can a style of architecture be found which traces its descent in an unbroken line from aboriginal American sources; this unique and valuable heritage is worth stressing."

Originally the Palace area was a fortress enclosed by an adobe wall. Inside were the palace itself, several small governmental buildings, and quarters for soldiers. The enclosed area within the wall was 400 feet long east-west and more than 800 feet long north-south. The Palace has undergone numerous renovations, and the wall and other buildings are no longer present.

Today the Palace of the Governors occupies the entire north side of the plaza, and it is fronted with a wide portal supported by wooden posts and corbels. Indians use the portal floor to display and vend their jewelry and pottery to tourists. The building is a one-storeyed, flat-roofed structure, in the shape of a rectangle around a central open patio.

Indians occupied the Palace during the Pueblo Revolt (1680-1692), and sixty successive Spanish governors ruled from this edifice. Later, from 1846 to 1907, it was the home of American territorial governors. Now it is a museum of history, and a visit to the exhibits inside will greatly enhance your appreciation of the nature and chronology of our settlement geography in North America.

The Palace of the Governors and the plaza form the heart of Santa Fe. A city zoning ordinance – well-known to historic preservationists and urban planners nationwide

This unusual view of the Palace
of the Governors gives you a sense
of what Santa Fe used to be like
before it was "discovered" by
twentieth-century artists, writers,
and tourists – a dignified old
Spanish town in repose. Completed in 1610, a full decade
before the Pilgrims landed
on Plymouth Rock in Massachusetts, the Governors Palace is the
oldest government building in
the United States. For centuries
Indians have used this site to ply
their cultural wares. Photograph
by Cotton Mather.

– restricts structures in the downtown historical zone to Spanish-Pueblo or Territorial architectural styles and limits building heights and types of signs. The heart of Santa Fe, with its other significant buildings, such as the Museum of Fine Arts on the northwestern corner of the plaza and the famous La Fonda Hotel (once a Harvey House) on the southeastern corner, constitutes one of the most esteemed places of our nation. It is bound to register indelibly with you, both culturally and historically.

Chimayo

• • • •

Chimayo is a famous old Spanish weaving community. Located twenty-five miles north of Santa Fe and eight miles east of Española, it was established shortly after the Pueblo Revolt of 1680–1692 on a site that had been occupied by Tewa-speaking Indians. The settlement, at an elevation of about 6,100 feet, is in a small picturesque valley lined with cottonwoods that is tributary to the Rio Grande. Most of the houses are on modest, semi-subsistence landholdings with patches of vegetables, beans, corn, and chile and with peach and apple orchards.

OF RELATED INTEREST: *River of Traps: A Village Life*, by William deBuys and Alex Harris (1990).

The community is frequented by visitors from afar who are aware of the nationally famous Chimayo weavings. Two weaving shops are especially renowned, Ortega's and that of John Trujillo. But much weaving is done by both youth and adults on large and small floor looms in the homes of the villagers. The weavings of John and Carlos Trujillo and their family members are internationally prized, and many are on exhibit in leading American, Far Eastern, and European galleries. John Trujillo is an authority on the history of weaving in this area. Fine hand-loomed, woolen textiles have been produced here since the early eighteenth century.

It is important to remember that the Indians had no sheep until the Spanish introduced them. The Spanish had a direct influence on the woolen textile designs that the Indians adopted in the Southwest. The similarities between the contemporary Hispanic and Indian designs are strong

John Trujillo (right), renowned Chimayo weaver, and Professor Cotton Mather (left) have known each other for decades. Here they share a few light moments under the snow-covered portal of Señor Trujillo's weaving shop. Photograph by George F. Thompson.

and are reminiscent of many hand-loomed patterns extant in Mexico. Many persons favoring Southwestern aesthetic motifs recognize these design interrelationships and are thus attracted to the woolen weavings of Chimayo.

El Santuario de Chimayo is another prominent attraction. This religious edifice, constructed between 1813 and 1816, has an interesting interior with closely spaced vigas, tin candelabra, and religious paintings. The sanctuary is noted as a healing place. In an anteroom are many crutches and canes, some from pilgrims who flock here on foot at Easter. The building is a flat-roofed structure with twin belfries, and it is set behind an adobe wall with an arched entrance. A small *acequia* (irrigation ditch) and large cottonwood trees *(alamosa)* nearby lend a simple rustic charm to the setting.

This distinguished century-old adobe home, belonging to Hermengildo and Trinidad Jaramillo, was converted in 1965 into the Restaurante Rancho de Chimayo, well-known for its regional decor and cuisine. Photograph by Cotton Mather.

The Jaramillo family has had a profound influence on Chimayo. The 1880 home of the family is now the Restaurante Rancho de Chimayo, one of the most charming eating establishments in the Southwest. Its exterior dining terraces, Hispanic culinary delights including great sopapillas, and interior decor retain much of the original allure of the Jaramillo home. Across the road from the restaurant is the Hacienda, a century-old Jaramillo residence now operated as a bed-and-breakfast hostel with rustic antiques of this village community and other amenities.

Santa Clara Pueblo ◆ ◆ ◆ ◆

The present Pueblo Indians are descendants of the Anasazis who lived over a vast area of the Colorado Plateau. They had established there a sedentary, hierarchial

Prior to World War II, Fred Harvey tour buses brought visitors here to the center of Santa Clara Pueblo. Pottery was displayed and sold on the ground under the two trees on the right. Most pottery today is sold within a potter's home. Photograph by Cotton Mather.

society and lived in complex communal structures. Agriculture was a mainstay of their existence. Their development on the Colorado Plateau had attained a peak in the thirteenth century. Drought and other factors forced some of the Anasazis eastward in stages to the Bandelier area and onward to Puye and thence to the Rio Grande valley (see page 53). This movement included the ancestors of the Santa Clara Pueblo. The Santa Clara Indians were at their current location when the Spanish arrived.

Today the Indian pueblos total nineteen – eighteen in New Mexico plus the Hopi in Arizona. In terms of population Santa Clara is a midsized pueblo. The two largest, Laguna and Zuni, have more than 6,000 persons each. The two smallest, Picuris and Pojoaque, have fewer than 300 each. Santa Clara has about 1,500 persons on the reservation; in 1790 their population numbered 134.

The advent of the Navajo, Apache, Comanche, and Ute Indians in North America came ages after the Pueblo Indians. The Navajo, Apache, Comanche, and Ute Indians are of different linguistic stock and are very distinct culturally from the Pueblo Indians.

Santa Clara Pueblo is located immediately south of Española. Its land today totals 45,744 acres. This is approximately four times larger than that held by the smallest pueblos, San Juan and Pojoaque, yet only one-tenth that of Laguna's.

Santa Clara's reservation has five major assets today: its prime location for employment in nearby Santa Fe, Los Alamos, and Española; its considerable area of alluvial land along the Rio Grande; its broad range of topography from valley land to highlands with mountain streams; its vegetative variety from xerophytic associations to the tall pines of Santa Clara Canyon; and its remarkable ancestral ruins within its reservation at Puye.

In the pre-Spanish period the main crops of the Santa Clara Indians were corn, beans, cotton, squash, and tobacco. The Spanish introduced cattle, sheep, goats, horses, burros, and chickens; also, they added crops such as wheat and barley, some vegetables, deciduous fruits, and melons. Food supplies before the modern period were augmented by gathering wild plant materials and by fishing and hunting. Both men and women worked at farming and gardening. In addition, women cared for the children, did household tasks, and made pottery. The Santa Clara people joined in the Pueblo Revolt against the Spanish from 1680 to 1692. Later, in 1821, their pueblo become part of the Republic of Mexico. In 1846 this area became United States territory.

Santa Clara is presently famous for its beautiful pottery. No other pueblo makes as many ceramics or excels it in quality. Both red and black pottery are produced, as it is in the nearby and much smaller pueblo of San Ildefonso. In addition, Santa Clara is noted for its carved pottery. Teresita Naranjo makes the finest: her pieces have won international acclaim. She sells her pottery exclusively from

Famed potter Teresita Naranjo works on one of her carved pots. Teresita writes: "A special kind of clay is found right here in the Pueblo where I live, about three miles away on a hill. First I bring home the clay and then let it dry outside for about two weeks. After the clay is dry, I soak it; then I sift some sand and mix them together. I find just the right kind of sand eighteen miles from my home." Photograph by Cotton Mather.

her home, much of it on order even before it is made! Numerous other potters of great distinction work in the pueblo as well.

Decades ago, pottery at Santa Clara was sold in a distinctive way. When a visitor's car appeared on the plaza, children playing outside would scamper to their homes with the news. Soon women would appear with pottery in baskets and spread it under a shade tree. The visitor would then examine the pottery and make choices. Today, the custom is to knock on doors of houses bearing "Pottery for Sale" signs and hope that someone is home.

In all of the pueblos except San Ildefonso, pottery is made and sold mainly by women. Most of the high-quality pueblo pottery is made in Acoma, Hopi, San Ildefonso, San Juan, Santa Clara, and Zia pueblos. Acoma, however, in recent years has become highly commercialized and crowded with tourists. Although some fine pottery is still produced there, much of it is no longer handmade; rather, it is factory-produced elsewhere and Acoma designs are added later to the exterior. Tourists have overrun both Acoma and Taos pueblos, and San Ildefonso is succumbing now to the lure of tourism.

Modern tourism has wrought distressing changes on some of the pueblos. Pottery traditions have been wrenched, some pueblos have been degraded into "living museums" or theme parks and are losing their community customs, some have risked their heritage on gambling casino tables, some dances have become roadside shows rather than being religious ceremonies, kivas and cemeteries have been crassly disrespected, and video- and camera-laden tourists have proceeded as though they were in a zoo. Santa Clara Pueblo, however, is an exception. Tourists are accommodated there effectively and with dignity. The Santa Clara Indians are aware of change, but strive to preserve their cultural identity and heritage.

Visitors should be cognizant of the Eight Northern Indian Pueblos organization, which is headquartered in San Juan Pueblo, three miles north of Española. This organization is an outgrowth of cooperative intertribal activities

A CLASSIC: *American Indians of the Southwest,* by Bertha P. Dutton (1903).

The headquarters of the Eight Northern Indian Pueblos organization is in the San Juan Pueblo, amongst tall cottonwoods. Nambe, Picuris, Pojaque, San Ildefonso, San Juan, Santa Clara, Taos, and Tesuque are the pueblo members of the organization. Photograph by Cotton Mather.

that began in the 1960s. It provides community services, fosters the preservation of the cultural environment, and sponsors the Annual Eight Northern Indian Pueblos Artist and Craftsman Show. This is the largest Indian-owned arts and crafts show in the Southwest. The 1994 show, for example, was held on July 16 and 17, near the entrance to Puye Cliffs. Dances are performed, photography and videography are allowed for a fee, parking is free, and fine pottery is on display for sale.

The Puye ruins and the Santa Clara Canyon are outstanding attractions of the Santa Clara Pueblo. They are professionally administered and maintained. Tours of the ruins are arranged, and the canyon has fine spots for camping, fishing, and picnicking. Puye was the prehistoric home of the Santa Clara Indians and was lived in from about A.D. 1450 to the late 1500s.

Santa Clara Pueblo is organized into two "moities" which govern both human and spiritual matters. Each moiety nominates the governor of the pueblo on an alternating-year basis. Business of the pueblo concerns that with the outside world, upkeep of the irrigation system, rental of pueblo property to outsiders, and regulation of grazing rights. During the Spanish period the pueblo was sustained by gathering, hunting, fishing, and farming. Today it is mainly sustained by wage work and pottery making.

OF RELATED INTEREST: *Storyteller*, by Leslie Marmon Silko (1981).

The modern Santa Clara Pueblo is one of the most representative, accessible, and noncommercialized of the nineteen contemporary pueblos. A visitor there has much to appreciate.

Bandelier Ruins and Monument ◆ ◆ ◆ ◆

The Bandelier ruins represent one of the milestones in the historic eastward movement of Pueblo culture from the Colorado Plateau to the Rio Grande valley. From the early A.D. 900s to the twelfth-century Pueblo culture, crop production, and commerce flourished at the great urban centers such as Pueblo Bonito in Chaco Canyon in northwestern New Mexico (see page 10). New forms of multistoreyed buildings emerged as a result of evolving masonry techniques; extensive trade was conducted regionally and interregionally, leading to important cultural and artistic exchanges; distinctive Cibola black-on-white pottery was made; and pioneering irrigation methods allowed for a prosperous agriculture.

With such bounty, however, came a burgeoning of population, and when a severe and prolonged drought hit the area during the twelfth century there was pressure to emigrate, especially to locations to the east that offered reliable sources of water and opportunities for agriculture and shelter. This movement from the Chaco region was gradual and ongoing, ending in the sixteenth century. Bandelier was a significant intermediate stop on the way to the broad, fertile valley of the Rio Grande.

At Bandelier you get out of the car, or bus, to explore the rich cultural and natural landscapes of this national monument. Photograph by Joseph Courtney White.

Bandelier is part of the Pajarito Plateau, which was formed by lava fissures, lava flows, tuff, and ash from volcanic activity in the nearby Jemez Mountains, including Valle Grande (see page 55). The plateau is cut by many gorges and canyons, such as Bandelier's Frijoles Canyon, which were made by tributary streams to the Rio Grande, such as Bandelier's Bean Creek, or El Rito de los Frijoles. The fertility of the soil in the canyon, the abundant game and rich bottomland forests, the protective cliffs, and the availability of building materials made Bandelier an enticing area for settlement. Settlement began as early as the twelfth century and ended around the mid-1500s.

Like their ancestors in Chaco Canyon, pueblo dwellers at Bandelier were farmers who grew beans, corn, and squash alongside Bean Creek in Frijoles Canyon and on mesa tops. Like their ancestors they chose well the locations for their houses and religious chambers. Villages paralleled the lush canyon creek and protective cliffs. They comprised impressive, irregularly terraced dwellings of masonry, from one to three storeys high, which, in the case of the large pueblo of Tyuonyi, contained 400 rooms plus kivas. Rooms were also carved out of the cliffs, which were often made possible by enlarging natural alcoves. And like their ancestors at Chaco, Bandelier's inhabitants were skilled artisans.

WORTH READING:
The Delight Makers, by
Adolph Bandelier (1890).

The ruins and, subsequently, the national monument (1916) are named for Adolph Francis Alphonse Bandelier, famed archaeologist and ethnologist of Swiss parentage and education. From 1880 to 1886 Bandelier carried out pioneering research studies, excavation, and surveys of pueblo architecture and culture in New Mexico, and part of his time was spent living and working in the ruins at Frijoles Canyon. His work on pueblo culture as well as on ancient civilizations in Mexico, Bolivia, and Peru became the foundation for future research in anthropology and archaeology in the United States.

Today Bandelier National Monument contains nearly 33,000 acres, two-thirds of which are designated wilderness areas. The combination of phenomenal natural features and remarkable pueblo ruins make this park one of the real treasures of the Southwest.

Valle Grande ◆ ◆ ◆ ◆

Valle Grande (Big Valley) is the site of one of nature's largest calderas. The caldera, which is an enlarged volcanic crater, has a diameter of more than twelve miles and comprises more than 176 square miles. Created by a series of catastrophic volcanic explosions, small resurgent domes formed within the crater from subsequent volcanic activity, as did lakebeds on the bottom of the depression. The caldera's floor is about 8,500 feet elevation, and the former volcano reached a maximum elevation of about 14,000 feet prior to the eruptions about 1,000,000 years ago.

Even a photograph taken with a medium-format camera can only hint at the scale and beauty of Valle Grande, one of the world's great calderas in high country that formed from a series of cataclysmic volcanic eruptions in geologically historic time. Massive explosions in modern time include Vesuvius (A.D. 79), Krakatoa (1883), Bondai-San (1888), and Mount Katmai (1912). Valle Grande compares in size with Crater Lake, the well-known caldera in the Cascade Range of Oregon. Photograph by George F. Thompson.

Valle Grande is in the Jemez Mountains, a broad uplift in the Southern Rockies. Composed primarily of igneous rocks, the area is highly faulted and contains numerous hot springs, including the famed ones at Jemez Springs. This lofty Valle Grande section extends into impressive highland country with tall ponderosa pine and alpine meadows. N.M. 4 runs along the south rim of the caldera.

Today this area is mostly under federal ownership. In colonial Spanish times, however, the land was divided into huge land grants and given to prominent families, such as that of former U.S. Senator Joseph Montoya.

Taos ••••

The small town of Taos is an enchanting place, and long has it been so. It has a spectacular physical setting and embraces a curious blend of five cultures: Hispanic, Anglo, Indian, the art and literary world, and the ephemeral tourist. Furthermore, it is enhanced by having three distinct geographical nodes, each with its own special appeal. Central is the Spanish town of Don Fernando de Taos, now simply referred to as Taos (population 4,065), and three miles to the south is the old Indian farming and residential community of Ranchos de Taos (population 1,779); the third node is Taos Pueblo (population 1,187), two miles north of the plaza.

Taos, astride the Rio Grande Rift that extends north-south from about Leadville, Colorado, to Juarez, Mexico, is on a plateau at 7,000 feet elevation. It is just twelve miles southwest of lofty Wheeler Peak, in the Sangre de Cristo Mountains — at an elevation of 13,161 feet, the highest point in New Mexico — and eight miles east of the Rio Grande gorge, where the river has cut 650-foot-high vertical walls into the plateau's basaltic lava. Small wonder that this setting has inspired many talented artists and that D. H. Lawrence proclaimed: "I think the skyline of Taos the most beautiful of all I have ever seen in my travels about the world."

In the recently renovated plaza at Taos you cannot help but be impressed by the memorial to the World War II dead. Photograph by Cotton Mather.

The resident population of Taos is about fifty-six percent Hispanic, six percent Indian, with most of the remainder Anglo. But Taos has a huge nonresident population and it is upon them that Taos is mainly dependent.

The Taos Pueblo has been in existence since the mid-fourteenth century. Spanish settlement at Taos was initiated in the seventeenth century. Anglo trappers and traders arrived in the early 1800s. Painters started coming in impressive numbers about 1890, followed by writers and photographers. Famous persons who have lived in Taos include Kit Carson, Ernest L. Blumenschein, D. H. Lawrence, Georgia O'Keeffe, Mable Dodge, and Ansel Adams. Now Taos is one of America's major art centers and it is the residence of literati and antiquarians. The excellent skiing nearby is, also, bringing new tourists to Taos.

The Church of St. Francis of Assissi at Ranchos de Taos was built in 1772. It has become, in the twentieth century, standard fare for some of America's greatest photographers and artists, but usually from the back side. Photograph by Cotton Mather.

The heart of Taos is the old plaza, with its covered bandstand, broad walkways, and shaded benches. Around the plaza are art galleries, studios, boutiques, restaurants, and the famous La Fonda Hotel. Narrow streets, old adobe buildings, and huge cottonwood trees make Taos most picturesque. The town is small, so the best way to explore it is simply by strolling.

The Taos Pueblo appeals to the image most Americans have of the Indian Southwest. This image has developed as the spectacular multistoreyed, communal, adobe architecture has been endlessly painted, photographed, and described in books and magazine articles. In fact, however, this pueblo is not typical of the contemporary nineteen pueblos, and it has become highly commercialized: the roster of tourist fees for visitation, parking, photography, and videography is long. Further commercialization is involved as numerous Indian vendors ply wares of limited curio value and Taos pottery, which generously can be described as having a certain rustic quality.

Ranchos de Taos has one marvelous attraction, the Church of St. Francis of Assisi. This elegantly simple adobe building is 120 feet long and has two beautiful bell towers and walls that are four feet thick. Many are the artists, including Georgia O'Keeffe, Paul Strand, and Ansel Adams, who have painted and photographed this building.

IN RETROSPECT: *North American Ethnology, Volume IV, House and House-Life of the American Aborigines,* by Lewis H. Morgan (1881).

The Lodge atop the Sacramento Mountains

• • • •

The Lodge in Cloudcroft, the focus of one of New Mexico's significant places, is set atop the pine-forested Sacramento Mountains that hover over the Tularosa Basin to the west (see page 63). This mountain range trends north-south and is the eastern limb of an immense anticline (layered rock arch). The San Andres Mountains constitute the western limb of this anticline. The Tularosa Basin is the collapsed portion of the arch, and it is a part of the Rio Grande Rift.

The main approach to the Lodge is via U.S. 82 from Alamagordo (Spanish for large cottonwood). This highway, from its junction with U.S. 54 near Alamogordo (elevation 4,400 feet), ascends to 9,000 feet in twenty-seven miles through vivid vegetative zones, past apple orchards and groves of cottonwood. Lithologically, the climb is through Precambrian granite at the mountain base and then through the overlying Paleozoic sedimentary strata, as exposed in the route upward in Fresnal Canyon. This scenic drive, with its panoramic views and tunnel, is along the nearby path of an old, abandoned cog railroad. This railroad was constructed in 1899 as a branch line of the Southern Pacific Railroad to secure timber for the mining interests centered at El Paso, Texas, some ninety miles to

From U.S. 82 you can see, especially during wintertime, an impressive wooden trestle on the abandoned cog railroad of the Southern Pacific's branch line from El Paso to Cloudcroft. Photograph by Cotton Mather.

the south-southwest. Shortly thereafter the New Mexico legislature dedicated 2,300 acres for a summer resort. The Lodge was the remarkable nucleus of this resort.

The original Lodge was constructed in 1899 by the railroad. It featured a fine restaurant, a dance pavilion, a billiard parlor, a children's playground, tennis courts, burro trips, a bowling alley, and the nation's highest golf course. A fire destroyed the main building on 13 June 1909. It was rebuilt by 1911 and now is one of the really elegant historic mountain retreats in the American Southwest. The Lodge was managed in the 1930s by the famous hotelier, Conrad Hilton, who, incidentally, was raised in San Antonio, New Mexico, the town between Socorro (see page 65) and Bosque del Apache (17). Many famous individuals have visited this distinctive retreat with its antique furnishings, comfortable accommodations, and superb view over

The front entrance to The Lodge at Cloudcroft, a year-round resort for those who enjoy high altitudes and historic settings. Photograph by Cotton Mather.

the white sands of the Tularosa Basin. Formerly the Lodge was known primarily as a highland refuge from the high temperatures of the adjacent lowlands. The average July temperature of El Paso, for example, is 81.4°F., whereas that of Cloudcroft is 59.7°F. Today the Lodge is popular in winter as a ski resort.

A fine side tour from the Lodge is southward along the splendid crest of the range to the renowned National Solar Observatory at Sunspot (elevation 9,200 feet). This observatory has equipment with a resolving power equivalent to reading an automobile license sixty miles away. The observatory, formerly under the auspices of the Association of Universities for Research in Astronomy, is a research facility available to foreign scientists and is visited by an educated citizenry.

More than a half million people annually visit the White
Sands National Monument, which is only a part of the
world's largest gypsum dune field (about 282 square miles).
This dunefield has formed in the Tularosa Basin (9,000
square miles), a large bolson (interior drainage area) or depression which formed as a downdropped block (graben)
of the earth's crust between the San Andres Mountains (ris-
ing to 8,239 feet), on the west, and the Sacramento Mountains (elevation more than 9,000 feet) and Sierra Blanca
Peak (elevation 12,003 feet), on the east.

Gypsum is a hydrous calcium sulphate that water has
brought in solution into this arid basin, with about seven
inches average annual precipitation. Winds, so characteris-
tic of desert climes, have heaped this glistening white gypsum sand into barcans as well as diverse parabolic and
transverse dunes.

The desert floor of the basin has mesquite, creosote
bush, saltbush, and grass, as well as playas (intermittent
saline ponds or lakes) such as Lake Lucero at the southwestern corner of the monument. Lake Lucero sometimes
holds ten square miles of very shallow water.

North of White Sands is the Malpais, a 120-square-mile
basaltic lava flow. East of White Sands are Alamogordo
(population 29,107) and the Holloman Air Force Base,
headquarters of the White Sands Missile Range (3,200
square miles), where the first atomic bomb was exploded
on Earth, 16 June 1945 at 5:29:45 A.M. Mountain War
Time.

The Tularosa Basin area is the home of an amazing variety of animals, including rabbits, foxes, lizards, mustangs,
and rodents. In addition, the oryx – a large African ante-
lope – was brought into the area about 1970 by the New
Mexico Game and Fish Department and now numbers
more than 1,000 head. The National Park Service consid-
ers this ravenous beast a menace to the Monument's native
plants and animals.

The Nuclear Age began here at Trinity Site, a National Historic Landmark, where the first nuclear bomb was detonated on 16 July 1945. The original photograph by Peter Goin is in color.

White Sands National Monument, in the Tularosa Basin east of the San Andres Mountains, features remarkable gypsum dunes and desert vegetation. Shoes are recommended during daylight hours. Photograph by Cotton Mather.

Settlers established ranching in the Tularosa Basin more than 100 years ago. Ranchers, however, were abruptly and ignominiously removed in 1942; the atomic bomb blasted off their hopes for a postwar return. Although the Army told the owners they could reclaim their land once the war ended, ranchers are still displaced, and the u.s. Court of Claims in 1989 rejected a request by 100 or so ranchers for about $50,000,000 in compensation. So visitors will not see these ranch operations today. You can visit, under government surveillance, the Trinity bomb site, located in the Jornada del Muerto (see page 20), but only on two days each year: the first Saturday in April and the first Saturday in October.

Also visible in the Tularosa Basin, along u.s. 70 between Alamagordo and Tularosa, and north of Tularosa along u.s. 54, are impressive new orchards of pecans and some pistachios. Tularosa (elevation 4,520 feet; population 2,615) is a charming town with attractive vegetation that was initially settled in the early 1860s by about 100 farming families from the Mesilla Valley who were displaced by floods along the Rio Grande. In 1979 the original forty-nine blocks of the townsite became a registered historic district.

OF RELATED INTEREST:
Nuclear Landscapes, by Peter Goin (1991).

Socorro ◆ ◆ ◆ ◆

Socorro, on the Camino Real from Mexico City to Santa Fe, is the major urban center in the southern part of the Rio Abajo (Lower River) region; to the north of the Rio Abajo region is the Rio Arriba (Upper River) Spanish settlement region. These two regions have been demarcated by scholars Alvar W. Carlson, in *The Spanish-American Homeland: Four Centuries in New Mexico's Río Arriba* (1990), and Richard L. Nostrand, in *The Hispano Homeland* (1992). It is clear now that a third region of Spanish settlement existed along the Rio Grande in a more recent period — what Cotton Mather calls the Rio Reciente region, which extends from the Rio Abajo south to El Paso, Texas, on the u.s.-Mexico border.

The plaza at Socorro will remind visitors of the Old Town Plaza in Las Vegas, New Mexico. Photograph by Cotton Mather.

Socorro (elevation 4,585 feet) is on an older alluvial surface of the Rio Grande, near the base of Socorro Peak (elevation 7,243 feet). This peak and the adjacent highlands have yielded silver, gold, lead, zinc, and copper. The Spanish had enslaved Indians here before the Pueblo Revolt of 1680 for the mining of silver, just as they had on the Turquoise Trail (see page 36). The big mining era, however, came after new silver deposits were discovered in 1867. Mining bustled until the 1890s. The Socorro smelter closed in 1895, the year that Congress demonetized silver. Socorro had boomed during the feverish mining-smelting period between 1867 and the 1890s. Indeed, during the 1880s Socorro was New Mexico's largest city, with forty-four saloons and slightly more than one person per foot of elevation above sea level.

The San Miguel Mission of the
Rio Reciente region at Socorro is
worthy of painterly renditions.
Photograph by Cotton Mather.

Socorro's population now is 8,159, and it is an architectural museum of ancient adobes as well as buildings of Territorial, Pueblo, Victorian, and Queen Anne styles. The latter two types became popular with the late-1800s mining boom. Many of the buildings are in need of restoration, yet a fine array exists within walking distance of the remarkably pleasant and shaded plaza known as Kittrel Park.

Most tourists race along Interstate 25 or go through Socorro on dreary California Street (old u.s. 85). Nearby, however, are such notable landmarks as the Garcia Opera House, the Illinois Brewery, the Crown Mill, the Socorro County Courthouse, and the San Miguel Mission. The courthouse, built in 1940, is an attractive edifice of Spanish-Pueblo style. The San Miguel Mission was constructed between 1819 and 1821 on the site of the Church of San Miguel, built in 1598.

A real oil rig is an appropriate sculpture for the campus of New Mexico Institute of Mining and Technology in Socorro. Photograph by Cotton Mather.

Socorro's principal claim to fame, however, is the New Mexico Institute of Mining and Technology, which opened in 1889. The 320-acre campus is abutted by a spectacular eighteen-hole golf course. The institution has one of the nation's outstanding mineral collections, the renowned Petroleum Recovery Research Center, and the New Mexico Bureau of Mines and Mineral Resources. The latter is the state's best source for obtaining good maps of New Mexico. The institution, with an internationally staffed roster of faculty and researchers, is one of the world's leading schools of mining.

Bosque del Apache, the renowned national wildlife refuge, is but eighteen miles to the south of Socorro via Interstate 25 and N.M. 1 (see page 17).

The old opera house on Main Street in Pinos Altos is an architectural historian's dream come true. Photograph by Cotton Mather.

Pinos Altos ◆ ◆ ◆ ◆

Pinos Altos (High Pines), seven miles north of Silver City, is a living relic of a gold-mining boomtown of the late 1800s. Three gold miners discovered placer gold there in May of 1860. By the end of the year approximately 1,500 fortune hunters – many from the Mother Lode country of California – had swarmed into Pinos Altos. The surging influx was opposed bitterly by the Apaches. Four hundred Apaches struck the town on 22 September 1861. Another battle ensued in 1866, but the inflow of fortune seekers persisted.

The boom started with gold panners along small streams getting ten to fifteen dollars' worth of the metal per day, but the surface ore was soon depleted. Then the lode ore was extracted; by 1890 this had peaked. A few mines, however, continued to be active until the 1920s.

Pinos Altos began as a ragged settlement of tents and shacks, but fortunes expanded rapidly. Grant County was formed in 1868 from Doña Ana County, and Pinos Altos briefly was the new county seat. In addition to gold, extractions were made of silver, lead, zinc, and copper. As fortunes accrued, the town mirrored prosperity and wild visions of the future. George Hearst, the father of publishing magnate William Randolph Hearst, was among the winners of fortune. The town soon had banks, saloons, an opera house, an adobe Methodist Episcopal Church funded by Hearst money, a hotel, and a store operated by frontier judge Roy Bean and his brother Sam.

Pinos Altos has resolutely persevered. The Methodist Episcopal Church now houses the Grant County Art Guild, the dirt streets are maintained, old miners' houses are presently occupied by artisans and craftsmen, memorabilia are sold, an ice-cream parlor proffers refreshment, and the old opera house stands as a monument to the past. A grave reminder for some is the old cemetery, and a geographical absurdity for this location is the full-scale model of the Santa Rita del Cobre Fort.

Santa Rita ◆ ◆ ◆ ◆

Santa Rita, about fifteen miles east of Silver City, is one of the world's largest open-pit mines. It is also one of the continent's oldest copper mines, having been worked by Indians in prehistoric times. Cabeza de Vaca learned in 1535 of the mineral deposit here when Indians presented to him a rattle made of copper. But it was not until 1804 that the Spanish started mining. At about this time, a Chihuahua banker, Don Francisco Elguea, purchased the property and, with a grant from the Spanish government, built the town of Santa Rita del Cobre.

The Apaches were less than enthusiastic about this entrepreneurial venture. Some of them had been captured and enslaved for labor in the mine. To maintain stability, the Spanish built a fort-prison. And close thereto they erected a church to lend a Christian aspect to the community. Yet

An old mine-head at the eastern end of the vast Santa Rita copper mine seems to keep watch over the tailings and the pit. If prices hold up, mining should continue here for another thousand years or more. Photograph by Cotton Mather.

the Apaches remained ruffled. So, in 1837, the Mexican government launched the Proyecto de Guerra (War Project) to liquidate the Apaches. The project included a government bonus to be paid for Apache scalps; the approximate equivalent was $100 per brave, $50.00 per squaw, and $25.00 per child.

The copper mined was high grade and was transported by mule train to Chihuahua, Mexico. It was reported that 20,000 mule loads were eventually transported, some of it onward from Chihuahua to the mint in Mexico City.

The Kennecott Copper Company obtained title to the property in 1873 from the heirs of Don Francisco Elguea, and the community expanded rapidly. The post office was established in 1881, and the population tripled between 1884 and 1915 to a total of 1,503 persons.

By 1910 the richer ores had been depleted, and open-pit mining began. Eventually the great mining pit enveloped the town, so the town was removed in 1950 and the townsite became part of the expanding mine.

The present-day mine is a spectacular sight. The mine rim is at an elevation of about 6,300 feet, and the pit is nearly two miles long, more than one mile across, and more than 1,200 feet deep. It is clearly visible even at 30,000 feet, on flight paths from El Paso to Phoenix and beyond. Gigantic trucks and shovels operate on broad benches and terraces that are connected with inclines to the rim. Until recently a viewing platform was available near the highway for tourists; now, with the ongoing expansion of the pit, the mine extends to the very edge of the highway.

The immense waste dumps of the Santa Rita mine are southeast of Silver City, at Bayard. Between the dumps is the leaching plant; from here the precipitate goes still farther south to Hurley to be smelted. In another millennium, conservationists may be roaming through the nearby Gila wilderness as the archaeologists and preservationists wax enthusiastically over the Santa Rita ruins!

The Gila ◆ ◆ ◆ ◆

When the Spanish, Dutch, Fenno-Scandinavians, and other pioneers and refugees from Europe landed on the Atlantic coast for good during the sixteenth and early seventeenth centuries, America was not yet a firm idea for the nation it would become. It was still largely a great wilderness area sparsely settled by diverse groups of "Native Americans" who had arrived on the continent tens of thousands of years ago in successive stages from Asia via the Bering Strait.

After colonial settlement was established, the American frontier was generally a westward movement across a series of "great divides": first, beyond the coastal plains of the Atlantic across the Piedmont and the Appalachians (Indians be damned), then beyond the Mississippi River across the

The Catwalk in Whitewater Canyon near Glenwood was used as a sanctuary by Apaches and their leaders during the U.S.-Apache wars. The stream later became an important source of mill water at the mining town of Graham after gold and silver were discovered upstream in 1893. Because the stream dried up in spots, four-inch and eighteen-inch pipelines were built in the canyon to tap a regular water supply for the mill. Men who climbed the pipeline to repair it dubbed it "the catwalk." The mill closed in 1913, the mines shut down by 1942, and the Catwalk became a National Recreation Trail in 1978. Recent "improvements" to the trail be-

came necessary when tourists "discovered" this previously unspoiled wonder of nature and human ingenuity. What once was a sanctuary is becoming a semi-congested tourist spot, especially during the peak summer season, thanks to good notices in the environmental and travel magazines.

The Catwalk is located in Catron County (6,898 square miles), which is larger than the states of Connecticut and Rhode Island combined. But with only 2,563 full-time county residents, elk now outnumber people by at least three to one, and elk are known to amble down the main street of Reserve, the county seat.

This was not always the case. By 1900 excessive hunting had ex-terminated elk and other wild game in New Mexico, which had to be reintroduced by the state. Today bagging an elk in Catron County is big business for local guides and some politi-cians. Photograph by George F. Thompson.

Children and adults enjoy rafting down the Gila River near the town of Gila. The 630-mile-long river, with headwaters in the Mogollon Mountains and Black Range of western New Mexico, is tapped for recreation, irrigation, and power all the way to Phoenix, Arizona. Photograph by George F. Thompson.

Great Plains (again, Indians be damned), and finally across or around the Front Range of the Rockies all the way to the Pacific Ocean. Some areas in the Interior West were skipped over by this American frontier "culture of development." One of the last big areas of wild country that remains relatively unplundered is thus found in New Mexico, in a region we call The Gila, and it took a visionary to make it what it is today.

Aldo Leopold, the great ecologist and conservationist who was a founder of the Wilderness Society and who proposed a land ethic for the United States and all nations of the world as early as 1933, began his career as a u.s. Forest Service scientist based in nearby Springerville, Arizona. He came to know the Gila well – its mountains, rivers, streams, and valleys, its vegetation and wildlife, its prehistoric dwellings and settlements, and its mining, logging, and ranching history – and he deemed it to be one of the special places left in America. In 1924, after he had left the Forest Service to become a professor at the University of Wisconsin-Madison, Leopold succeeded in having portions of the Gila National Forest designated as the first extensive wilderness area in the United States, forty years before Congress passed the Wilderness Act!

Since 1924, when the wilderness area was set aside, America's population has more than doubled, and the end is nowhere in sight. So little remains of the original domain, in fact, that the few remnants of wild country – such as the Gila – take on increasing importance for a modern populace confronted with crime, traffic, stress, and all the other social problems affiliated with suburban and urban life. Americans now yearn for, and are even desperate for, retreats and second homes in rural settings, and those with money are gobbling up real estate in the remote portions of the Interior West as if they are eating French fries. The American frontier, it turns out, is alive and well, only under a different guise.

The Gila, therefore, presents Americans and New Mexicans with at least two great challenges. How can the Gila, as one of America's more important areas of wild country, survive the onslaught of a tourist trade even as the towns that depend on the Gila – such as Glenwood – openly sell land for recreational and retirement homes? And when do we, as a nation, realize that tourism itself is as great an environmental threat as unscrupulous mining and logging of past times that "ecotourists" complain about?

The Gila is much more than a wilderness area; it is an *idea* about *place*. Just consider what actually comprises the Gila: the Gila Wilderness and the Gila National Forest, to be sure, but also the Gila Cliff Dwellings, the Catwalk, the ranches along the Gila and Sacramento rivers and in the Gila and Sacramento valleys, the town of Gila, and more. And consider that Geronimo, famed leader and warrior of a Chiricahua group of Apaches who gave the U.S. Army

OF INTEREST: *The Gila: River of the Southwest,* by Edwin Corle (1951).

The Gila Cliff Dwellings in Catron County, part of the country we call The Gila. Don't be discouraged by the roadside billboards advertising these ruins: they remain a very special place to explore on foot. Uphill climbs are required. Photograph by George F. Thompson.

and Anglo settlers hell, lived as a boy in the upper Gila River valley, which was part of the Apache homeland.

The Gila is a special place that embodies the very essence of the interconnectedness between the natural and humanly constructed worlds. It is Leopold, after all, who proclaimed in *A Sand County Almanac* (1949): "That land is a community is the basic concept of ecology, but that land is to be loved and respected is an extension of ethics." Let us hope we don't love the Gila to death.

Carlsbad Caverns ◆ ◆ ◆

Mammoth Cave National Park in Kentucky and Luray and Endless Caverns in Virginia are the focus of attention for many tourists and would-be cavers in the eastern United States. In the American West, people head to Carlsbad

Caverns alongside the Pecos Valley in southeastern New Mexico. How the caverns came to be is an interesting story.

Some 250,000,000 years ago this area of the Southwest was part of a vast, shallow tropical ocean, the Permian Ocean, that featured a 400-mile-long, horseshoe-shaped reef – Capitan Reef. This ancient marine fossil reef, which extends into present-day west Texas and New Mexico, is one of the finest on earth, and you can readily see the fossils exposed in the beautiful Guadalupe Mountains National Park, which was established in 1966.

Carlsbad is located at the northern edge of Capitan Reef. After the shallow sea evaporated, the reef subsided, became buried by sediments, and was then uplifted by the same forces that begot both the Rocky Mountains (elevation to 14,431 feet) and the Guadalupe Mountains (elevation to 8,751 feet) some 60,000,000 years ago; the caverns were then formed by water over time in the thick limestone that developed in the shallow extension of the sea. Limestone is a rock that is formed chiefly by the deposition and consolidation of the skeletons of marine invertebrates, and most caves are found in limestone areas because limestone is soluble in water.

The spectacular stalactite and stalagmite formations for which Carlsbad is world famous were created recently, in the last 500,000 years, when small seepages of water found their way into the by-then dry caverns, evaporated, and left a deposit. Stalactites hang from above; stalagmites build up from the cavern floor. When the two join they are said to form a column.

Discovery of the caverns is attributed to cowboy Jim White and his pal Abijah Long in 1901, though other settlers at an earlier time had made preliminary forays into possible cave entrances. Artifacts found in the caves, however, date back 12,000 years, so we now know that prehistoric Indians, as well as Apache, used the caverns for shelter and as a cool retreat. The temperature in the caverns is a constant 56°F. Cowpunchers, guano miners, speleologists, park rangers, and tourists came after the "discovery," which reminds us that when Columbus discovered America

A park ranger at Carlsbad Caverns National Park prepares to escort visitors underground to one of the natural wonders of the world. The nearby Guadalupe Mountains are also spectacular for their marine fossils, wildlife, and great diversity in vegetation – from desert-floor fauna to big aspen and tall pine at higher elevations. Photograph by Cotton Mather.

for Spain in 1492, coincidentally this was the same year the Indians discovered Christopher Columbus.

Be that as it may, Carlsbad Caverns is renowned not only for the size of its chambers and the beauty of their formations, but also as a breeding ground for millions of bats, the most numerous being the Mexican freetail (*Tadarida brasiliensis*). The bats emerge each evening from late spring through October to feed on insects. They prefer the tropics during the winter.

Bat guano was mined initially by Jim White and other ex-cowboys-turned-miners via a large iron bucket that was lifted on a cable 170 feet in an engineered mine shaft from the deposits. Efficiency soon improved after a modest underground ore railway was constructed, though the mining never realized memorable profits. The peak of production came in 1933 when nearly 100,000 tons of the fertilizer were removed from the cave by the Carlsbad Bat Guano Company, mixed at a nearby plant, and shipped to southern California for use in the emerging citrus industry there. Operations ceased by the time of Pearl Harbor.

Carlsbad's potential as a tourist attraction was recognized when it became a national monument in 1923 and a national park in 1930, even as mining of the guano continued. The surface area within the park has grown from 700 acres to 46,774 acres. Seven miles of trails are lighted, and the perimeter of The Big Room, the largest chamber, at 754 feet below the surface, is an amazing 1.25 miles long. We still don't know how extensive the caverns are: at last count there were seventy-six separate caves, making the caverns already among the largest and most impressive on earth. But recent discoveries of new caves with one-of-a-kind features (open only for scientific purposes) encourage scientists and authorized cavers to explore even more of the great beyond in a remarkable underground place called Carlsbad Caverns.

Fort Selden and Fort Selden Springs

••••

Fort Selden, fourteen miles northwest of Las Cruces as a sober crow (*Corvus sobrius*) flies on Sunday, was built in 1865 near the east bank of the Rio Grande. Its purpose was to protect settlers from Apache raids. This specific location along the Rio Grande Rift is in the narrow sector that separates the Mesilla and Rincon valleys. The Mesilla and Rincon valleys are broad, downdropped block portions of the valley of the Rio Grande which have deep alluvial deposits. The narrow intervening portion of the Rio Grande flowage between the Mesilla and Rincon valleys forced traffic between the hills. Apaches found that these hills and the riverine terraces were strategic spots for launching attacks.

Fort Selden, situated on a terraced upland, was a complex of flat-roofed adobe structures surrounding a parade ground. Approximately 200 men were stationed at the fort,

The necessity for ruins becomes evident at Fort Selden. Photograph by Cotton Mather.

and they quickly quelled Apache depredations. So the fort was abandoned in 1878, only to be reopened in 1880 to secure the advancing track of the Santa Fe Railway along the Rio Grande. Captain Arthur MacArthur was the post commander in the 1880s; his son, Douglas, of World War II fame as a general, spent several years of his boyhood at this outpost. Fort Selden is today a state monument with a fine historical museum and an interpretative trail through the ruins of the fort.

One mile north of the fort, along the diversion canal and over the narrow short bridge at the dam, are the Fort Selden Springs, now known as Radium Springs. The present name of the springs evolved from the radium reported in the water. These springs were used formerly by the Indians, later by the Spanish, and subsequently by the military personnel at Fort Selden.

A LITERARY CLASSIC:
The Sea of Grass, by Conrad Richter (1937).

The Harvey House Hotel at Fort Selden Springs, now known as Radium Springs, originally had a great location for lodging and dining. Photograph by Cotton Mather.

A Harvey House Hotel was built alongside the railroad and by these springs in the early 1900s. Fred Harvey had conferred with officials of the Santa Fe Railway in the 1870s and had induced them to establish a network of hotels and dining rooms to serve the travelers of that era. The women employed were known as Harvey Girls; most of them were Midwesterners, aged eighteen to thirty, and from poor families. Harvey Girls were highly trained as hostesses and waitresses. They were chaperoned in dormitories and meticulously uniformed. They were single and had to remain so while under contract to Fred Harvey.

This was at a time when there were "no ladies west of Dodge City and no women west of Albuquerque." Harvey Girls thus provided a respectability and a refinement to railway travel, and the network of Harvey House hotels and restaurants achieved national acclaim. The Harvey

House at Fort Selden Springs was one of this larger group of great travel facilities that enabled Americans and foreign visitors to appreciate the Southwest in comfort and style. Renowned Harvey House hotels in New Mexico included ones at Albuquerque, Clovis, Gallup, Lamy, Las Vegas, Santa Fe, and Vaughn.

Associated with the Radium Springs or Harvey House Hotel were a large swimming pool and a bathhouse. The temperature of the water is 140°F; it no longer flows, and must be pumped. The hotel is now in a dilapidated state. Between 1978 and 1982 it was leased to the state of New Mexico as a women's prison. Later it was briefly operated as a Hungarian restaurant. Today it is enclosed by a high, barbed-wire and chain-linked enclosure with a locked gate and a threatening sign – a sad monument to a bygone elegant edifice near historic Fort Selden.

OF RELATED INTEREST: *The Harvey Girls: Women Who Opened the West,* by Lesley Poling-Kempes (1989).

Mesilla ◆ ◆ ◆

Mesilla (Little Tableland) is a nationally known small community in southern New Mexico, redolent of its Mexican heritage. This area was in Mexican territory when the town was officially formed in 1853. At that time Mesilla was on the west side of the Rio Grande. Across the river on the east side was the American town of Las Cruces.

The Gadsden Purchase agreement in 1854 provided for a territorial transfer. This was formalized on the Mesilla plaza as the Mexican flag was lowered and the flag of the United States, with its thirty-one stars and thirteen stripes, was raised.

By 1858 Mesilla, with a population of 3,000, was the largest urban place between San Antonio, Texas, and San Diego, California. It was the trade center of the productive Mesilla Valley, the regional name for the irrigated Rio Grande lowland between El Paso and Fort Selden (see page 79) that today is known for its extensive pecan orchards. Mesilla, also, was a stop on the Butterfield Overland Mail route between St. Louis and San Francisco. The town had fashionable dress shops, farm-supply stores, a church, street fairs, a theater, and other urban amenities such as cockpits and bullfights.

The Rio Grande changed its course in 1865; now it flows west of both Mesilla and Las Cruces. The edge of the old riverbed is visible on the right as one travels on Avenida de Mesilla (N.M. 28) from the Interstate 10 exit to the town of Mesilla.

During the Civil War Mesilla was occupied first by Confederate troops and then by Union forces. Today, however, the town's historic focus is, sadly, on Billy the Kid. He was tried here in 1881 at the courthouse on the southeastern corner of the plaza and was sentenced to be hanged for the murder of Sheriff William Brady. Billy the Kid described Mesilla as the "worst place he had ever struck." This utterance has an enduring appeal to residents of rival Las Cruces. The Kid was taken to Lincoln, now an historic district, ten miles northwest of Hondo, where he made his last escape. He was killed a few months later by Sheriff Pat Garrett near Fort Sumner. Thus ended the escapades of another capricious folk hero of the American West.

Crucial to the history of Mesilla was the decision in 1881 of the Santa Fe Railway to lay its route through Las Cruces instead of Mesilla. Today Las Cruces proper has a population of 65,000 and growing, second largest in the state, whereas that of Mesilla has only slightly more than 2,000. Las Cruces now is the epitome of a bustling, modern American city of the Automobile Age with little as a reminder of its past, whereas Mesilla preserves its architectural heritage, its old *acequias* (irrigation ditches), and its original street patterns. An annual fiesta on the plaza commemorates Diez y Seiz de Septiembre (September 16), Mexican Independence Day.

Mesilla is one of the most distinctive towns in the Southwest. Many of its people are bilingual and are descendants of Mexicans who settled there in the mid-nineteenth century. They are proud of their ancestry and have resisted palpable attempts of sprawling Las Cruces to absorb them. Mesilla, also, has fended off all nationally fran-

Today nearly 1,000 fewer people live in La Mesilla than in 1858, though most remain bilingual. Mesilla remains one of the great places in the Land of Enchantment, and the plaza serves as the center for this old Hispanic enclave. Photograph by Cotton Mather.

chised businesses, and it has no main street lined with motels, gas stations, fast-food joints, supermarkets, gaudy billboards, multistoreyed office structures, or glitzy neon signs. Instead, as you enter town on N.M. 28, you will find festive stands for the selling of *ristras* (strings of chilies), a well-designed boulevard with appropriate regional landscaping, and an attractive gallery of art.

The town's core is the sedate old plaza with its attractive gazebo and antique, wrought-iron benches under pleasant shade trees. Around the plaza are arcaded sidewalks of one-storeyed structures, built long ago, and the twin-towered cream brick church that dominates the north side. On the east side is the Double Eagle Restaurant, with its elegantly furnished interior; this building was originally a sumptuous residence with a beautiful interior patio. On the southern and southeastern edge of the plaza are the renowned La Posta and El Patio restaurants, which feature Mexican fare with excellent chile. Both restaurants are housed in buildings of historic significance. An extraordinarily fine bookstore on the west side of the plaza is replete with regional volumes.

Gems such as Mesilla inevitably gain wide recognition. So, today, many wayfarers include this living legacy of bygone times in their itinerary, and Mesilla has added quite an assortment of boutiques, most of which are in harmony with the cultural setting. The ultimate question, however, is a familiar one: Can Mesilla maintain its historic and aesthetic character and sense of community amidst a tourist onslaught? This is the constant concern of the town's government and its board of trustees. For the moment Mesilla is a special place; with vision and planning may it so remain.

INDEX

General Index

Unless otherwise noted, all towns and cities listed herein are in New Mexico. Ornaments (•) indicate a registered place. Page numbers for main entries are in *italics*.

ABOUT THE AUTHORS

Cotton Mather (left) and George
F. Thompson (right) at Bosque del
Apache National Wildlife Refuge.
Photograph by Stuart Klipper.

COTTON MATHER is founder and president of the New Mexico Geographical Society, a nonprofit organization dedicated to the public welfare. He is a former chairman of the department of geography at the University of Minnesota and he has held fourteen other professorships at
distinguished universities in the United States, Canada, and overseas. He
has authored and coauthored half a dozen books, most recently *Beyond
the Great Divide* (Rutgers University Press, 1992), coedited an award-
winning atlas of Kentucky, and published dozens of articles in leading
American and foreign professional journals. In addition, he cofounded
America's oldest county geographical society, owned and operated a renowned gallery of vernacular art in the Twin Cities area, demonstrated
the world's first portable television, and, during World War II, served as
an editor in the Army Map Service, as a research analyst for the Office of
Strategic Services, and as a lecturer for the Army Specialized Training
Program. Professor Mather has worldwide field experience, including
expeditions to the High Arctic and the Andes. He is a former member of

The Explorers Club, New York City, in recognition of his Mount Everest expedition with Professor P. P. Karan, famed Himalayan scholar. His travels in New Mexico date back to the 1920s. Professor Mather's Tewa Indian name, *Sahaun-povi* (White Cotton Flower), was conferred upon him by a former Pueblo governor. He lives and works in Mesilla, New Mexico.

GEORGE F. THOMPSON is founder and president of the Center for American Places, a nonprofit organization based in Harrisonburg, Virginia, and Mesilla, New Mexico, that is dedicated to enhancing the public's understanding of geography and place, especially through books. He previously worked as an acquisitions editor for John Hopkins University Press, was a founding editorial member of *Landscape Journal* and *The Black Warrior Review*, and has taught on numerous occasions at The Colorado College in Colorado Springs, the University of Wisconsin-Madison, and other institutions of higher learning. He is editor of *Landscape in America* (University of Texas Press, 1995), coauthor of *Beyond the Great Divide* (Rutgers University Press, 1992), and founder and director of the *Creating the North American Landscape* series (Johns Hopkins University Press). Books he has developed and brought to publication have won or shared nineteen major prizes, including the PEN Center USA West's Literary Award for the best book of nonfiction published in the United States. Born in Colorado, Mr. Thompson has traveled extensively in New Mexico and the American West throughout his life. He has lived in the Shenandoah Valley of Virginia since 1983.

ABOUT THE SOCIETY

The New Mexico Geographical Society, legendary society of the American West, is a nonprofit organization dedicated to the public welfare. It fosters the discovery and dissemination of geographical knowledge far and wide through public lectures, regional and international conferences, educational field trips, research, and publications designed to reach the student, scholar, and general reader. Its headquarters are in La Mesilla, the historic community in southern New Mexico that was under the jurisdiction of the Mexican State of Chihuahua until the 1854 acquisition of the Gadsden Purchase Territory by the United States. For information about membership, events, and Society publications, please write:

The New Mexico Geographical Society, Inc.
P.O. Box 1201
Mesilla, New Mexico 88046-1201
U.S.A.

REGISTERED PLACES OF NEW MEXICO

Volume One in the *Registered Places of America* series

Designed by Glen Burris.

Set in Monotype Columbus, a typeface drawn by Patricia Saunders. Based on printing types used in Spain during the early 1500s, Columbus was designed for the quincentenary of Christopher Columbus's voyage of 1492 to the New World.

Printed and bound by Thomson-Shore, Inc.

Library of Congress Cataloging-in-Publication Data

Mather, Cotton, 1918–

    Registered places of New Mexico : the land of enchantment / Cotton Mather and George F. Thompson.—1st ed.

       p.   cm.—(Registered places of America; 1)

    Includes index.

    ISBN 0-9643841-0-8 (alk. paper)

    1. Historic sites—New Mexico—Guidebooks. 2. New Mexico—Guidebooks. I. Thompson, George F. II. Title. III. Series.

F797.M37   1995

917.8904'53—dc20   95-15897